EUROPE'S BEST BAKERIES

Over **130** of the finest bakeries,
cafés and patisseries across
Great Britain and the Continent

SARAH GUY

september

The idea for *Europe's Best Bakeries* began simply, with an interest in a fast-expanding baking scene – one of the few areas of the high street that is truly flourishing – and an admiration for the individuals driving the growth.

Food writer and editor Sarah Guy enlisted top restaurant reviewers, food and travel writers, and baking and food bloggers from throughout Europe to search out and review the best bakeries, large and small. The results are combined with photographs both from the bakeries themselves and from a host of enthusiastic Instagrammers and bloggers, creating what we hope you'll agree is a feast of a book.

This book is dedicated to all those who are brave enough to follow their passion and rise at 3am to knead our breads and mix our cakes.

CONTENTS

By Country

Introduction

There are 135 life-enhancing bakeries, patisseries and tearooms in this book, and there could have been hundreds more: so many traditional establishments continue to thrive, and the revival of interest in real baking has meant scores of new bakehouses across Europe.

Real bread is staging a fight-back after years in the doldrums and regaining its place as 'the staff of life'; bakers from different countries are exchanging ideas and practices, new ideas are being introduced and ancient grains are being rediscovered. Both the longevity of Europe's finest patisseries and the popularity of *The Great British Bake Off* demonstrate that there will always be an appreciative audience for the artistry and creativeness involved in baking.

Every bakery has a story to tell. Sometimes it's an individual one, about a baker or cake-maker on a personal crusade, but often there's a bigger tale, with regional histories and cultures captured in recipes and baking lore. We've visited small, family-run bakeries producing the same wholesome loaves as 100 years ago, historic grand cafés showcasing impressive cakes made to centuries-old recipes and single-minded modern bakers inspired by the magic of sourdough. Opening a patisserie or a bakery is rarely about simply finding a retail niche – the life of a baker, while satisfying, is just too hard (those early mornings) to undertake without real enthusiasm. Premises big enough to hold ovens, a shop and perhaps even a mill are expensive, especially in cities, where even railway arches don't come cheap. Passion isn't a word used in many professions, but it's one used all the time when baking is involved. Many of the bakers featured in this book have an almost missionary zeal about the life-enhancing properties of real bread, while pastry chefs have always known about the pleasure that a perfectly executed patisserie can bring.

Real bread, made with flour, water, starter and salt, and left to rise naturally, will do most people nothing but good, just as – in moderation, of course – a slice of exquisite gateau as an afternoon pick-me-up is a joyous thing. For those who cannot tolerate real bread, many of today's

bakers are extending their talents to gluten-free baking, and some establishments, such as Chambelland and Isabella Glutenfreie Patisserie, produce only gluten-free goods.

Sourdough bread and fancy doughnuts may be popular all over Europe, but many other baked goods remain resolutely regional: there's a thrill to trying tsoureki in Thessaloniki, cuarto in Mallorca or croquants in Nîmes. There's also something satisfying about going to the source: buying biscotti at Biscottificio Antonio Mattei in Prato, Italy; deciding which Lisbon pastelaria makes the best pasteis de nata; or visiting a stroopwafel specialist in Amsterdam. *Europe's Best Bakeries* lists all these glorious treats and more, and is a reminder that bread, cakes and buns are almost as much fun to read about as to consume.

Choosing which bakeries to include was a challenge. We wanted to feature much-loved community favourites as well as publicity-savvy big names, and to list inspiring new bakeries alongside historic boulangeries and patisserie-cafés, including idiosyncratic single-item producers and one-man bands along the way. Scores of excellent bakeries missed the cut, so apologies if your favourite Parisian patissier or London sourdough maestro isn't here. Suggestions came from all over Europe, from bakers themselves as well as enthusiastic customers. The reviews were written by food and travel writers, baking and food bloggers, and restaurant reviewers, all knowledgeable consumers of baked goods, and some of them also skilled practitioners.

We've listed the reviews alphabetically to make it easy to find a favourite bakery (for listings by country, see the Contents), and also to immerse the reader immediately in the wealth and variety of baked goods available across Europe. So Maison Adam, a specialist macaron producer, sits next to Maison Aleph, a brilliant new French-Syrian fusion patisserie; the Old Post Office Bakery, an old-school organic bakery, follows Oberweis, one of Luxembourg's smartest establishments – all fascinating, mouth-watering and unique examples of Europe's long and impressive baking tradition ◦

TH

BAKE

IE
RIES

Åpent Bakeri

Oslo, Norway

📍 Damplassen 24-25,
0852 Oslo, Norway
🔖 apentbakeri.no

When Øyvind Lofthus and Emanuelle Rang opened Åpent Bakeri on Inkognito Terrasse in 1998, they changed Oslo's bakery scene forever.

When Øyvind Lofthus and Emanuelle Rang opened Åpent Bakeri on Inkognito Terrasse in 1998, they changed Oslo's bakery scene forever. The pair combined French and Norwegian baking traditions to splendid effect, and their first artisan bakery introduced wonderful croissants and French bread to the capital. The Åpent French country loaf represented a departure from Norwegian baking norms; even today its deep brown crust and moist crumb gives the competition a run for its money, and it's served in many of Oslo's best restaurants. Both the bolle (the much-loved Norwegian take on a cardamom bun) and the baguette are served with jam from Sogn, the well-known berry-producing district of Norway, on the side. Thirteen openings later, this handsome, airy spot at Damplassen is a favourite hangout with locals. It's in a refurbished old bakery, in a green, well-heeled area of the city away from the tourist trail. Coffee comes from Oslo-based Lippe, a renowned *kaffebrenneri* (coffee roaster), and is best enjoyed with one of Åpent's croissants (fabulous, flaky, buttery things) or the famous bolle – a divine combo, and the epitome of Scandinavian *hygge*. A variety of sweet options includes brownies, slices of apple cake, pasteis de nata, scones, fruit tarts and a wealth of seasonal treats. There are loaves aplenty, plus sandwiches (open and filled, with the likes of shrimp and dill mayo) and lunchtime salads. On a summer's day, kick back with a homemade ice cream or sorbet at one of the outdoor tables – prime territory for watching the world go by ◉

Aran

Dunkeld, Scotland

📍 2 Atholl Street, Dunkeld,
   Perthshire PH8 0AR,
   Scotland
⚲ aran-bakery.com

The bakes continue to fly off the shelves, and it's not unusual for all the sourdough loaves to have been sold by noon.

What used to be a down-at-heel newsagent's in the pretty Perthshire village of Dunkeld hit the headlines when it became Flora Shedden's *aran làthail* ('daily bread' in Scottish Gaelic). Shedden, who shot to fame after she made it to the semi-final of the BBC's *The Great British Bake Off* in 2015, used her new-found status to raise funds for her very own bakery, and it's turned out to be a real star. When it opened in October 2017, everything sold out in four hours. Even now, the bakes continue to fly off the shelves, and it's not unusual for all the sourdough loaves to have been sold by noon, especially on a Saturday.

'Flora bakes as much as she can herself,' smiles Scott, who like many of the staff that work at Aran, went to Dunkeld school with Shedden, and can account for her reputation as a hard-working and gifted artisan, 'but demand has been so high that she's had to rent out another unit, in Birnam, where the bakers can get on with much of the preparation of the cakes and pastries.' Nearby Birnam is the site of the famous oak – the last of the Birnam Woods that famously moved to Dunsinane on the helmets of soldiers to fulfil the witches' prophecy in *Macbeth* – which means that there's no shortage of Shakespeare pilgrims. Visitors stock up on picnic supplies – though you can perch at a window seat for a coffee and a croissant, there's no full-scale café as yet.

In terms of daily bread, the bestseller is the classic sourdough, but *GBBO* fans tend to make a beeline for the leaf-shaped fougasse, a Provençal version of focaccia with a lovely scattering of herbs and salt. There's also a walnut and honey rye – just perfect for weekend mornings with coffee and the newspapers.

Many of the ingredients that go into the cakes and sandwiches – free-range eggs, meats and salads – come from local producers, which further elevates Aran's standing in the community, as do the distinctively Scottish specials: one popular sweet pastry is the Fly Cemetery (a sweet, crumbly fruit slice) and the shortbread is, of course, exemplary. But Flora's talents run to more exotic cakes too: there's the tonka bean and rhubarb cake, for example, or the black sesame and vanilla one, alongside the more familiar brownies, cookies and scones ●

Aromat

Warsaw, Poland

📍 Ulica Sienna 39, 00-121 Warsaw, Poland

🕊 aromatpiekarnia.pl

You can see the bread being baked: kids enjoy peering through the glass and seeing the staff in action.

A winning blend of Polish and French baking, opened in 2015, Aromat was the homecoming project of a Polish family based in France. As Maciej Adamczyk was finishing his MBA, his mother had just completed her diploma in patisserie at a prestigious Parisian institution. 'Rather than hang it on the wall,' says Adamczyk, 'we decided to set up our own business back home.'

This modern café-cum-bakery right beneath the gleaming Warsaw Towers in the centre of the city exudes warmth and a pride in quality produce. Every two months or so, a lorry arrives from Paris carrying stone-ground French flour, and often it also brings over a French expert to school Aromat's bakers in the ways of slow fermentation. You can see the bread being baked: kids enjoy peering through the glass and seeing the staff in action, though their attention soon wanders to the bright

display of eclairs (pistachio, nut and vanilla, lemon and chocolate).

A recent introduction, inspired by a trip to Stockholm, has been cinnamon rolls. 'My mother's always getting ideas when she travels,' laughs Maciej. The lemon cake (there's also an orange variety) is a riff on the US-style carrot cake. Polish tradition hasn't been forgotten either. Classic dark and rye breads sit alongside the baguettes (classic and rustic), while the 100 per cent Arabica coffee is roasted in Warsaw (there's a house blend in the pipeline). The formula is a success: as well as a thriving wholesale business supplying nearby offices and hotels, there's another branch of Aromat at the trendy Hala Koszyki food market, and yet more in development ○

Auguszt

Budapest, Hungary

Kossuth Lajos utca 14-16, 1053 Budapest, Hungary

auguszt.hu

The appearance of gesztenyepüré (chestnut purée) in the display cabinet signals the arrival of autumn.

Auguszt in name, august in appearance, this fifth-generation family concern located near the equally historic hub of Astoria is one of Budapest's most venerable *cukrászda* (patisserie). The foundation date of 1870, elegantly carved on the window, can only hint at the backstory here: upheaval, war, imprisonment, destruction, rebirth – and cakes.

Let's start with the cakes. Displayed around an island counter, itself the centrepiece of a two-floor interior filled with marble-topped tables, are delicacies old and new. Chilis mangó torta, a light mousse of mango with a touch of chilli and a biscuit base, is a contemporary invention. Auguszt krémes, three layers of thin wafer separating fresh cream and vanilla, would have been just as popular when Elek Auguszt unveiled his little pastry shop on the Buda side of the Danube in 1870. Fame spread after his son József

won top prize in the baking contest at Hungary's seminal millennial celebrations of 1896, and József and his wife opened another *cukrászda* with a terrace, garden and palm trees in 1922, sending their son Elemér to do his pastry training at the Dorchester in London.

Then war brought havoc. Elemér spent three years in a Soviet prisoner of war camp before struggling home to a bombed-out shop in 1948. His father found another location, living just long enough to see it succumb to the Communist takeover. After the 1956 Uprising, Elemér and his wife opened up on Fény utca, passing the business on to their son József.

In the 1990s, this downtown outlet was set up and given a vintage revamp to echo a century or more of tradition. Currently, granddaughter Auguszta runs the Pavilion branch near Farkasréti cemetery, while her sister Flóra oversees operations here.

Beneath a huge chandelier, savoury snacks, such as spenótos hassé (petite spinach pastries) and krumplis pogácsa (potato scones), share the spotlight with slices of apple pie and towering layered creations of Habsburg heritage. Beigli, synonymous with Hungarian Christmas, is offered year-round in its common poppy seed or walnut varieties. The appearance of gesztenyepüré (chestnut purée) in the display cabinet signals the arrival of autumn. All coffees can be ordered caffeine free, teas are loose-leaf, and there's a roaring trade in lemonade and ice cream in summer ◦

Bäckerei Balkhausen

Cologne, Germany

📍 Apostelnstraße 27, 50667 Cologne, Germany
📞 +49 221 2570264

More than eighty types of bread are formed and baked here every day.

Bäckerei Balkhausen may seem pretty busy during the week, but on Saturdays you have to queue down the street to get through the door of this Cologne institution. While you're in line, however, you can appreciate the bakery's window displays, with breads of all shapes and sizes stacked in one window, and a neat display of pastries and cakes in the other. Once inside this very traditional shop, you'll find it worth the wait: the small room is wall-to-wall with good-value artisan breads and pastries, the atmosphere is lively and welcoming and the smell (and view) of freshly baked goods being pulled out of the ovens and brought to the front of the shop is simply wonderful.

Service is very fast, yet friendly, even when the lines are out the door. Trained pastry chef Gerd Balkhausen believes his bakery's popularity is partly down to the sheer variety of products on offer. More than eighty types of bread are formed and baked here every day, and there are often new additions, sometimes from recipes suggested by Gerd's customers and employees. 'Variety is important,' he says, 'it keeps the customers interested.'

Popular loaves include the dark Dänische Schwarzbrot (Danish black bread), Kartoffelbrot (potato bread) and Möhrenvollkornbrot (carrot wholegrain bread); the vegetable quiche is also very good. The sweet stuff here should not be overlooked either, from the moreish Russischer Zupfkuchen (part chocolate cake, part cheesecake) to the wonderfully sweet and nutty hazelnut yeast-dough Bobbes. During carnival season, you can hardly move for what many consider to be Cologne's best Berliner (jam filled doughnuts).

Among the extraordinary selection of breads and pastries here, there's one that's particularly special – not just to the bakery, but to the city of Cologne itself. During World War I, Vice-Mayor Konrad Adenauer (who later became the first Chancellor of West Germany) patented a recipe for an emergency bread, made using a high percentage of corn flour as rye and wheat were scarce at the time. Much later, Gerd modified Adenauer's recipe, using whole grains of corn instead of flour, and today he's the only baker in the city still selling Kölner Brot (Cologne bread) •

Bäckerei Hinkel

Düsseldorf, Germany

◉ Hohe Straße 31, 40213
Düsseldorf, Germany
⚲ baeckerei-hinkel.de

Mandelhörnchen (almond crescents), Nussecken (nut wedges) and Quarkbällchen (deep-fried quark batter balls dusted with sugar) all make perfect snacks.

Düsseldorf's favourite bakery was founded in 1891 by Jean and Katharina Hinkel. Having been handed down through three more generations of the same family, the business is now run by their great-grandson Josef, who is also the head of the Düsseldorf's guild of craft bakers. Electing to focus on quality and service, the Hinkels have only ever had two outlets, located just 300 metres from each other in Düsseldorf's old town, not far from the river Rhine.

Hinkel's Hohe Straße bakery is home to their energetic baked goods production. It's a warm and welcoming shop with a bustling atmosphere, a classic German bakery that offers a couple of standing tables if you want to snack inside, but not an awful lot of room for much else. There are rustic-looking loaves in the window and classic German cakes and pastries in glass counters.

Loyal customers come from near and far, but the friendly staff are efficient, so you never have to wait too long to be served.

The baked goods at Hinkel's are very traditional, very high quality, and very, very German. The loaves and bread rolls are made almost exclusively of wheat, spelt and rye, plus their own natural sourdough starters; all are produced by hand. Around sixty different kinds of bread are baked here each day, and there are various daily specials on top. Choose from rye and rye mixes, wheat and wheat mixes, alternative grain breads such as buckwheat, or the raisin breads – particularly good is the Wochenendstuten, or weekend raisin bread, dotted with almonds, raisins, candied lemon and orange. There's also a huge selection of rolls sprinkled with various seeds, and some top-notch savoury pastries such as the Athena,

a hearty wheat bun topped with sheep's cheese and hot peppers.

Browse the cake counter for a slice of cherry crumble cake or Butterkuchen, a yeast-dough cake made with a lot of butter, sliced almonds, sugar, marzipan and cream. Mandelhörnchen (almond crescents), Nussecken (nut wedges) and Quarkbällchen (deep-fried quark batter balls dusted with sugar) all make perfect snacks. At Easter and Christmas, don't miss out on Hinkel's Stollen, which contains a cheeky slug of Killepitsch, the local herb liqueur ⦿

Bäckerei Pfeifle

Freiburg, Germany

⟟ Carl-Kistner-Straße 20, 79115 Freiburg im Breisgau, Germany
⚑ baeckerei-pfeifle.de

Once you've got one of Pfeifle's breads or pastries in your hands, you'll be transported.

Situated on a main road in the Haslach district of Freiburg, the original Pfeifle bakery is thriving. It was founded in 1906 by Franz-Josef Pfeifle and his wife, Karoline. Four generations later, the business has survived two world wars and much economic hardship, and the enthusiastic Wolfgang Pfeifle is at the helm. Freiburg's favourite bakery has another ten branches in the city, plus a permanent farmers' market stall.

This outlet is a little bland, but the staff are friendly and efficient, there's adequate seating inside, and in any case, once you've got one of Pfeifle's breads or pastries in your hands, you'll be transported somewhere else altogether. The baked goods are made with real passion for both traditional baking craftsmanship and the city of Freiburg; ingredients are of the highest quality, and regional and seasonal wherever possible. Gourmet magazine *Feinschmecker* has named Pfeifle one of Germany's best bakeries every year since 2001.

Having become an active supporter of the Slow Food Association in 2009, these days Pfeifle is focused on giving the entire baking process more time and care. It's one of the first bakeries in Germany to use innovative volcanic stone ovens to produce a loaf with a crunchier crust and more delicate crumb. Stone oven-baked bread rolls include the Oberlindenweck, a crusty wheat roll made with fresh quark and semolina (also available in loaf and baguette forms), and the Augustinerweck, a rye roll with a deeply addictive flavour. In terms of loaves, the highly aromatic Friburger Michel is a must-try – a wheat sourdough bread with a delicate, splintery crust made to a secret recipe. The rustic Green City Einkorn, made with 100 per cent einkorn wheat (the oldest ancient grain in the world), is favoured for its nutty, honey-like flavour. The Puddingplunder, a Danish pastry filled with vanilla cream, is our pick of the plentiful sweet pastries ○

Bageri Petrus

Stockholm, Sweden

◉ Swedenborgsgatan 4b, 118 48 Stockholm, Sweden

☎ +46 8 641 52 11

Bageri Petrus could be described as the perfect blend of French patisserie heritage and old school Swedish home-baking traditions.

Petrus and Alexandra Jakobsson are the dynamic duo behind this little bakery in Södermalm, considered by many to be the best in Stockholm. It's an unassuming spot, more cosy than flashy, but once you sink your teeth into one of their buttery, crispy croissants, pains au chocolat or kouign amanns you'll realise what the fuss is all about.

Bageri Petrus could be described as the perfect blend of French patisserie heritage and old school Swedish home-baking traditions, with flavour and texture as the guiding principles. Creations come caramelised, crispy, nutty or creamy in just the right way; a mouthwatering mix of slightly sweet and the right kind of salty.

Choose between imported classics like pasteis de nata and canelés or go native with cinnamon buns and the 'seven kinds of biscuits' that were served at every respectable Swedish

coffee gathering right up until a few decades ago. Other Swedish evergreens are milanopinne (a biscuit filled with almond paste), pariservåffla (buttercream-filled wafers) and kongress (hazelnut-filled tarts).

Petrus Jakobsson also makes sensational bread (sourdough, of course). He loves to experiment with locally sourced and milled grains such as spelt and einkorn, and the bread is cold risen for flavour. The Danish rye brings tears to the eyes of expat Danes. The breads are named after streets in the neighbourhood – the levain

'St Paul' and the walnut bread 'Yxkull', for example.

The bakery has recently expanded to allow for more seating – although the business is mainly a bakery, many people have realised that it's also a charming location for a *fika* (coffee break). Don't expect Italian espresso coffee here, though – in keeping with the back-to-basics philosophy, the coffee is filter, but it is well-made and freshly brewed, from beans roasted by the micro roastery at Koppi. One final tip: if you're looking for a hearty breakfast, order the spelt porridge ◦

Bageriet

London, England

◉ 24 Rose Street, London
WC2E 9EA, England

⚓ bageriet.co.uk

Sit in here with a coffee and a sockerkringlor – a sweet, brioche pretzel that, like a good doughnut, leaves sugar round your mouth – and you have achieved *fika*.

This tiny café/bakery hits the sweet spot with a well-edited selection of Swedish buns, cakes and bread. Although Bageriet is located in the centre of Covent Garden, it's tucked down an alleyway, so finding it feels like unearthing treasure. The pretty window display suggests a haven of warmth and cinnamon buns. Inside there are fancy cakes and tarts: the mazarin (an iced almond tart), the hallankokos (raspberry and coconut) and the oddly-named dammsugare (vacuum cleaner cake), a little cylindrical cake covered in marzipan and chocolate. There's a range of Danish pastries, plus tartlets piled so high with fruit they resemble a virtuous option. Full-size cakes include a gaudy green princess cake (marzipan-covered sponge) and the nut-covered almond cake. Specials appear throughout the year: semlor (cardamom flavoured buns filled with almond paste and whipped cream) in the weeks before Easter, lussekatter (S-shaped saffron buns) during Advent. Savouries are limited to a few well filled rolls. The bread is excellent, too – a small range of loaves includes a white poppyseed bloomer and a Danish dark rye. It's worth paying Bageriet a visit for the blackcurrant rye alone – moist, fruity, equally good on its own or with cheese.

Amazingly, everything is baked downstairs in a space no bigger than the café – premises so cramped there's only room for two tables and a coffee machine. The white-painted space is given character by a few vintage pieces, including the Scandinavian sugar canisters, and shelves stacked with own-made granola, jams and crispbread and all manner of Swedish biscuits. Sit in here with a coffee and a sockerkringlor – a sweet, brioche pretzel that, like a good doughnut, leaves sugar round your mouth – and you have achieved *fika* ◉

Baker Tom

Falmouth, England

⚲ 10C Church Street,
Falmouth, Cornwall
TR11 3DR, England

⚑ bakertom.co.uk

He was one of the first on the artisan bread scene in Cornwall and he's now a household name in the area.

The Baker Tom story started over ten years ago, with two loaves of bread pedalled on Tom Hazzeldine's bike over to the local farm shop where he worked. His loaves proved popular, and before long he opened a small shop in Truro (now closed) selling his bread. He was one of the first on the artisan bread scene in Cornwall and he's now a household name in the area, with four shops around Cornwall and dozens of other stockists in the south-west (including, most significantly, Riverford organic grocery deliveries).

Yet, despite his successful trajectory and now extensive offering, Baker Tom continues to put the emphasis on simplicity. No tricks, no preservatives, no artificial additives or added sugar – a loaf of his traditional bread contains just flour, sea salt, fresh yeast and water. And everything is freshly made daily, by hand.

There's something pleasingly unpretentious about Tom's bakeries. The décor is simple and clean, and though the selection is constantly evolving (with seasonal specialities keeping things fresh – toffee apple hot cross buns, say, or festive fruit sourdough loaf), it isn't so *recherché* as to shun such everyday pleasures as a white tin loaf, a flapjack or a simple but well turned out wholemeal bread roll. In fact, Tom's stated aim is 'to make good bread an everyday choice' and his prices reflect this, being more accessible than many artisan bakers, and with unusually generous portions. As well as a variety of organic tin loaves, there are seeded spelt beauties, hand-shaped malthouse bread and long-fermented, basket-proved sourdough loaves in three styles (classic, seeded and malt).

Sweet treats are arranged with casual abundance in the window. The classic trio of French pastries (croissant, pain au chocolat, pain aux raisins) is present and correct but the talking points are favourites like the vast Kernow curl (Kernow is Cornish for 'Cornwall'); a spicy fruit bun made with an egg-rich dough, generously spread with butter and dotted with brown sugar and currants; lumberjack cake, made with apple and dates with a coconut topping, and a satisfyingly straightforward chocolate caramel flapjack.

The oversized soft and fluffy scones containing great chunks of cherry and fruit (there's also a cheese option) are some of the finest around and can be bought alongside jars of strawberry jam and the requisite tubs of Cornish clotted cream. The saffron bun – a Cornish speciality – is also suitably golden and distinctively spiced. Baker Tom's brioche burger bun is something special, and it's wrapped around many a burger in local restaurants.

Baker Tom bakeries sell a small but carefully chosen selection of other deli items, including speciality oils, meats, cheeses and Cornish sea salt, as well as breadmaking kits and loaf tins. At this outpost, café fare is also served – you can stop for a coffee with a pastry, a round of freshly made sandwiches or a bowl of soup with a hunk of bread ●

Baker's Table at Talgarth Mill

Talgarth, Wales

📍 Talgarth Mill, The Square, Talgarth, Brecon LD3 0BW, Wales

🔗 talgarthmill.com

Bara brith – Welsh bread made with dried fruit soaked overnight in tea – is a real favourite.

Not many bakers can say that all their flour comes from their local mill, but every loaf produced here uses wholemeal flour from the Talgarth watermill. The café and bakery at the Talgarth Mill complex are part of a community initiative; here you can also buy the work of over thirty artists and craftspeople, and the site is supported with the help of volunteers. The restored eighteenth-century watermill grinds three or four days a week, and a variety of wholemeal flours and breadmaking kits are available to buy. You can watch the mill in action or head straight to the Baker's Table for coffee (from James Gourmet Coffee in Ross-on-Wye) and cake. What's available changes regularly, but bara brith and scones with jam and cream are constants. Bara brith – Welsh bread made with dried fruit soaked overnight in tea – is a real favourite, and the scones often sell out. Otherwise,

there's a changing roster of cakes, which always includes a gluten-free option, not to mention coconut macaroons, brownies and blondies, plus seasonal treats such as stollen. The dishes on the short café menu use local ingredients in soups, salads and sandwiches (Carmarthenshire cheese with homemade red cabbage coleslaw, for example), whereas much of the herbs and soft fruit come from the mill's own garden. The ham and cheese sharing platter is deservedly popular, and a wood-fired oven is put to good use on pizza nights. The choice of loaves for sale includes white, granary, spelt and sourdough, but the bestseller is a white and rye mix known as bara havard. Take one of the Baker's Table breadmaking classes and see if you can make one anywhere near as good ◦

Bakeshop

Prague, Czech Republic

📍 Kozí 1, 110 00 Prague 1,
Czech Republic

↟ bakeshop.cz

Just as the first Bakeshop became
a convivial mid-morning hangout
for Prague's expat writers and artists,
so today's light-filled venue on Kozi
encourages customers to linger.

Though it was founded by an expat from New Jersey, there's far more to Bakeshop than bagels and cheesecake. Established by Anne Feeley beside Prague's Old Town Square, Bakeshop entered its twentieth year in 2018 as a thriving, two-outlet business. These days the main café, shop and bistro is this branch, near the Jewish Museum and Cemetery.

Feeley died in 2012, after passing her artisanal baking enterprise on to Martin and Carolyn Hofman. 'Many of our Bakeshop recipes are still from Anne,' says Martin, 'such as the old French sourdough ones from the training she did in France.'

Originally, Anne, unable to the find the specialty bread with nuts or dates she enjoyed back home, simply found a niche in the local market. Today the bakery continues to evolve, with less familiar breads given a showcase. 'Probably the most attractive is our walnut bread, but my favourite is our potato variety. It stays nice and moist.' It's one of Martin's own creations.

Just as the first Bakeshop became a convivial mid-morning hangout for Prague's expat writers and artists, so today's light-filled venue on Kozí encourages customers to linger over a slice of walnut and blue cheese quiche or a cinnamon yoghurt muffin. Sandwiches, say with a red pepper and pesto chicken filling, are made using their classic sourdough. Most sourdough types – walnut, black olive, rosemary and olive oil – are available by the kilo or half kilo, or simply as loose rolls (a rarity in Prague).

Though trends come and go (gluten-free options are currently much in demand) some cakes never go out of fashion. According to Martin: 'The popularity of our cheesecake, particularly the chocolate marble one, doesn't change whatever the season. Our carrot cake too' ⊙

Baltic Bakehouse

Liverpool, England

⚲ Baltic Triangle, 46
  Bridgewater Street,
  Liverpool L1 0AY, England
↡ balticbakehouse.co.uk

The big social media star is the 99, a doughnut filled with vanilla cream and crowned with a chocolate flake.

What many people hail as the best independent bakery in Liverpool was started in the city's Baltic Triangle by Brenda Henley, her daughter Grace and son Sam, gifted bakers all. The family now have two bakehouses, with the Allerton Road branch boasting a restaurant and café.

Bread is the big story at Baltic. The Baltic Wild, an oft-praised sourdough loaf, is a chewy, tangy revelation. The dough has fermented for at least ten hours and the loaves are made 'by hand, by eye and by intuition'. The family also sell yeasted breads, including an extremely popular soft batch, which goes by the name of Baltic Soft. This slightly honeyed wheatgerm bread is baked in a loaf frame, made from specially seasoned wood, which produces bread that's fragrant and springy, and delicious with butter.

As well as the loaves, there are pastries and croissants, pleasingly light and distinctive and the reason many a commuter takes the Baltic route to work. Another lure is the bacon sandwich, which, when made with Baltic bread, sets the bar to a whole new level. There's more sweet stuff in the form of custard tarts and cream slices, and a bakehouse special, Crack Pie (yes, named for its addictive qualities), a sticky, oat-based, slightly salt-caramel pudding/tart. Then there are the doughnuts, which practically have celebrity status. Baked fresh every day, the sugared, sweet orbs of dough are light and yielding. Most popular is the traditional jam, but Baltic also bake a lemon custard one that produces a lovely little edge of sharpness alongside the sweet. However, the big social media star is the 99, a doughnut filled with vanilla cream and crowned with a chocolate flake ◦

Barbakan

Manchester, England

📍 67-71 Manchester Road,
Manchester M21 9PW,
England
🔗 barbakan-deli.co.uk

The evocative aroma of freshly baked goods makes it near impossible to pass by without a purchase.

When a business is still thriving after fifty years, you know there's something special going on, and that's the case with Chorlton's much-loved Barbakan. The firm supplies many businesses in and around Manchester, and has won a raft of awards. Over the years, the Najduch family have turned the bakery and deli into a local attraction. While its roots are in Eastern Europe – it is named after the famed gateway in Krakow – the product range covers a much wider geography.

As you approach Barbakan, the evocative aroma of freshly baked goods makes it near impossible to pass by without a purchase. Make your way through the lively outdoor terrace, step inside, and, while you prepare for a bewildering set of options, make sure you collect a ticket (the queue can be a long one, sometimes out the door).

The range really is astonishing, with over seventy varieties of bread baked on the premises each day, from Irish soda breads to German Kaiserbrot (with rye flour) via Italian- and French-style loaves. The granary sourdough is a favourite – get there early if you don't want to miss out.

Breads aside, it's worth a visit just for the mouthwatering selection of cakes and pastries. There's something for everyone among muffins, doughnuts, shortbreads, brownies, Danish pastries, cheesecakes and tarts, but hardest to resist is the stunning poppy ring, icing and all.

The deli also sells cold meats, sausages, patés, cheeses, jams, pastas and sauces. Though primarily a shop, there's a café section too. A short but appealing menu offers hot and cold sandwiches (the New Yorker features pastrami with dill pickle, mustard mayo and salad), quiches and the like, plus good value teas and coffees ●

Beigel Bake

London, England

📍 159 Brick Lane, London
E1 6SB, England
🔖 beigelbake.com

Beigel Bake never closes – it's open twenty-four hours a day, seven days a week – and there's often a queue.

Beigel Bake may not be much of a looker, but its popularity comes from the deliciously chewy and generously filled bagels, not the interior décor. A modestly sized, functional looking room with a long counter gives way to a small bagel production room at the rear; more baking magic happens upstairs. The bagels are boiled before being baked, which gives them their unmistakable texture, and thousands of them fly out the door every day.

Beigel Bake never closes – it's open twenty-four hours a day, seven days a week – and there's often a queue. Have your order ready: the queue moves fast, and beware a sharp comment if you can't immediately ready reel off your request when it's your turn. The busy staff are briskly cheery with everyone from clubbers to tourists, but they don't have time to talk you through the menu.

You can buy a single, unfilled bagel for 30p, or several dozen for a party, or a heavily stuffed one to cure whatever ails you: smoked salmon and cream cheese is the perfect hangover cure; the mighty salt beef (with or without mustard, perhaps with a pickle) is dinner sorted. Egg mayo, plain cheese, and chopped herring are other popular fillings. As well as stacks of bagels, there are rye breads, challah, Danish pastries, apple turnovers and a dreamily good baked cheesecake. Drinks are limited, with the tea served in a Styrofoam cup, and if you eat in you'll be standing huddled in a corner, but this place is an institution. It's been here since 1974, a small reminder of the once-thriving Jewish community around Brick Lane, and it's hard to imagine London without it ●

Bertinet Bakery Café

Bath, England

⦿ The Vaults, 2 Brunel
Square, Bath BA1 1SX,
England

⚲ bertinetbakery.com

When it comes to the bread,
sourdough is king.

Bath is home to three venues run by expert baker and Brittany native Richard Bertinet: the Bertinet Kitchen is a school running breadmaking and cooking classes (it also opens as a shop on Saturdays); the Bertinet Bakery is in a narrow street in Bath's central shopping area and sells take-away coffee alongside the baked goods, and then there's the Bertinet Bakery Café, which sits under stone railway arches in the plaza outside Bath Spa station, with a few indoor tables along with outdoor seating. Copies of Bertinet's five books dotted around let customers know they're in the hands of a master, and Bertinet himself has become better-known thanks to TV appearances on *Saturday Kitchen*. Growing demand also led him to open a bakery in Milton Keynes in 2014, to supply delis and shops around the south of England, though bread for the bakery and bakery café is baked daily in Bath.

When it comes to the bread, sourdough is king. Like Bertinet's other varieties of bread, it's traditionally made without recourse to flour improvers or enzymes, and loaves are hand-moulded and proved in linen-lined proving baskets. The sourdough uses the special Bertinet ferment and comes with a heavy, chewy, crust with a hint of caramel, which is a lovely contrast to the slightly sour and moist interior. As well as classic bloomers, ciabatta, baguettes, spelt and levain-levure (a white loaf that includes some sourdough ferment), there are indulgences such as rosemary and rock salt focaccia. Bread is made daily and disappears daily – roll up near closing time and you're likely to find almost bare shelves.

The café does a brisk lunchtime trade (mainly take-away) in unpretentious savouries served from a warming cabinet – the likes of sausage rolls, quiches and filled croissants. But many customers are here for the cakes and pastries: an appetising array of viennoiserie sits alongside light-as-a-feather meringues, classic tangy French lemon tarts, lemon meringue pies, mille feuilles, madeleines and pear and almond tarts, and – veering away from the traditional French vibe – salted caramel brownies ⊙

Bettys

Harrogate, England

9 1 Parliament Street, Harrogate HG1 2QU, England

⚑ bettys.co.uk

Teatime treats are what the firm is known for, from delicate fondant fancies to stout fruit cakes.

Although Bettys tearooms seem as Yorkshire as can be, the business was started by a Swiss baker and chocolate-maker, Fritz Bützer. He anglicised his name to Frederick Belmont, and opened his first café in Harrogate in 1919 – no one knows why he chose the name Bettys – and another in York in 1936. Today, the Bettys tearoom chain is six strong, supplied by their craft bakery just outside Harrogate (where they also have a cookery school). It's still a family firm and, while a busy mail order service keeps far-flung fans happy, for the full Bettys experience, you have to come to Yorkshire.

All the tearooms have a shop attached, and each has its own character – art deco styling, some of it original, in the St Helen's Square branch in York, and a collection of vintage teapots in the Ilkley outpost, for example. The Swiss heritage is celebrated in dishes such as chicken schnitzel and the giant rösti, as well as in the sweet stuff. There are speciality tea blends and single origin roasts to drink – Bettys bought Taylors tea and coffee merchants in 1962.

All the baked goods served in the tearooms are produced by the Bettys bakery, including the bread, from the soup rolls to the steak sandwich stick. Teatime treats are what the firm is known for, from delicate fondant fancies to stout fruit cakes. There's a fixed afternoon tea, but it's much more fun to pick and choose from the menu. Northern treats include Yorkshire curd tarts, Eccles cakes and the Fat Rascal. This last item is unique to the bakery; created in 1983, it's a sort of cross between a scone and a rock cake, decorated with glacé cherries and almonds to create the 'rascal' face. The selection on the cake trolley changes daily, but might include a vanilla slice (puff pastry, raspberry jam and fresh cream vanilla custard), a fresh fruit meringue or a Swiss chocolate torte. Cold weather blues can be banished with a warm treacle tart, a buttered pikelet or some cinnamon toast. Or for something savoury, the Yorkshire rarebit, good on its own, can also be ordered with crispy bacon.

The bakery is big on seasonal goodies – at Easter there's everything from chocolate bunnies and Easter eggs to Simnel cakes on offer, while white chocolate ganache ghosts make an appearance at Halloween, and there's Yorkshire parkin around Bonfire Night. Be prepared to queue at peak times ●

Bewley's

Dublin, Ireland

📍 78-79 Grafton Street,
Dublin 2, Ireland
🔖 bewleys.com

The buns are still substantial hunks, glistening with sugary toppings and perfect with a big mug of tea or coffee.

Sitting in Bewley's grand café on Grafton Street with a cup of tea and a sticky bun is a time-honoured Dublin treat. The Bewley family were Quakers who came from England in the early 1800s and made a name for themselves in 1835 by bringing the first cargoes of tea from China to Ireland; today the firm (no longer family-owned) is Ireland's leading tea and coffee company.

The Grafton Street café opened in 1927, and the handsome set-up quickly became an institution. It saw some uncertain years, which ended when it closed in 2015 for what turned out to be a 12 million euro reconstruction. The premises reopened in late 2017 with a fresh look and layout that maintained many of the building's original features, while increasing table space (it now seats 500) across several floors.

The menu has also been overhauled, so the formidable cheese plate now comes with a variety of breads (all made on the premises), including Guinness and treacle bread, raisin and walnut, and a turmeric-infused sourdough. Soup and a scone could mean a bowl of hearty potato and leek served with a cheddar and chive scone or a tomato focaccia. Seafood stew comes adorned with a golden crisped puff pastry covering creamy fish and mussels, while the children's menu includes a chocolate and almond financier as well as a pain au chocolat.

Happily, some of the old favourites survived: the 'original' sticky bun, plus almond and cherry varieties top the cake list, and the buns are still substantial hunks, glistening with sugary toppings and perfect with a big mug of tea or coffee. The signature Mary cake, a flourless classic from 1945, with chocolate mousse and apricot on almond and hazelnut sponge, remains on the menu and sits comfortably alongside newer patisserie items such as matcha green tea and raspberry religieuse or Valrhona chocolate and berry delight. Take a seat, order a sugary pick-me-up from the smart waiting staff and enjoy the airy surroundings and glorious stained glass ●

Biscottificio Antonio Mattei

Prato, Italy

⚲ Via Ricasoli 20, 59100 Prato, Italy
⚑ antoniomattei.com

'Mattonella', as the shop is known locally, makes the best biscotti in the world, the benchmark against which all others are judged.

As the name suggests, biscotti di Prato – hard almond biscuits transformed when dipped in vin santo, sweet 'holy wine' – originated in Prato, a busy town south-west of Florence. They are ubiquitous in Tuscany, where they're also known as cantucci (though in fact the original cantucci were flavoured with aniseed, which biscotti di Prato are not).

Right in the centre of the medieval old town, stands the Biscottificio Antonio Mattei, the old-fashioned sign declaring it to be a *fabbricante di cantucci*. 'Mattonella', as the shop is known locally, makes the best biscotti in the world, the benchmark against which all others are judged. 'Mattei IS the biscotto di Prato,' explains Elisabetta Pandolfini, one of the present owners. The company was founded in 1858 by Antonio Mattei, who created a simple, hard biscuit made with five ingredients (flour, sugar, eggs, almonds and pine nuts) which soon became popular locally. He brought his biscuits to the Esposizione Italiana in Florence in 1861 and then to the World Fairs of 1862 and 1867 in London and Paris respectively. The biscuits won prizes at all three and their fame soon spread way beyond Prato. In 1908, the flourishing business passed to in-house baker Ernesto Pandolfini, and it is now run by his four grandchildren.

Production takes place right here, behind the elegant shop, where the inviting aroma of warm eggs, sugar and almonds greets you on arrival. Wooden shelves behind the counter are filled with biscotti in distinctive original deep turquoise packaging tied with string. It's still very much an artisanal affair – the family decided to eschew over-expansion and over-diversification in favour of quality and a handful of classic recipes. Biscotti are still made to the original formula, resulting in small golden chunks of hard, nutty, eggy perfection, although recently versions with chocolate and pistachio and almond have been introduced (hence the red and green packaging). Then there are the brutti buoni (literally 'ugly good' – chunky, sticky lumps of baked ground almonds and egg white), biscotti della salute ('healthy biscuits' – slices of toasted buttery brioche loaf), torta Mantovana (a pale, round sponge cake topped with toasted almonds) and the filone candito, a moreish brioche log studded with bright glacé cherries and wrapped in a fine layer of almond paste.

In 2018, a tiny jewel-box of a shop was opened in the centro storico of Florence; at the back is a small museum. Mattei now exports the biscotti to some thirty countries worldwide, but the heart of the business is, and will remain, in Prato ⊙

Black Isle Bakery

Berlin, Germany

Linienstraße 54, 10119 Berlin, Germany

blackislebakery.com

The cake is served in surprisingly hefty portions for such a sleek and sophisticated environment.

Its roots are Scottish, it arrived in Berlin via London, and it doesn't sell bread. The Black Isle Bakery is quite unlike your average artisan bakery: it looks much more like a gallery, with its stark white walls, grey polyurethane floor and gleaming copper benches.

The tag 'of London' adds an extra shot of cool to a name that reflects owner Ruth Barry's Caledonian heritage. She grew up on the highest point of the Black Isle peninsula, in the Highlands, and would no doubt have 'searched the skies for the Red Kite' as a wee girl. Such whimsical phrases in praise of the wild Scottish landscape are etched in blue lettering on the walls of her café, to be contemplated while sipping delicate White Forest tea from Panchthar, Nepal, or hand-roasted single estate coffee from Ethiopia, which trickles hot and strong from a gleaming, state-of-the-art espresso machine.

Having trained as an artist, Barry forged a career in the arts, before changing tack to refocus her creativity on baking by way of a gruelling three-month apprenticeship at the celebrated Du Pain et des Idées boulangerie in Paris. Her Black Isle brand went down a storm in London for a few years, before she decided to pack lock, stock and baking trays, and move to Berlin. Her gleaming bakery opened here in the autumn of 2017, to much acclaim.

All the food on the shortish menu is baked daily in the café's open plan kitchen and displayed artfully on a brass topped counter, the cakes assume loaf formation under glass, and the big, satisfying cookies inhabit Trendglas jars. Black Isle has also earned a place in Berliners' hearts with its exemplary weekday lunch options: buns bursting with wild salmon, crème fraîche and dill, and flaky pastry tarts with tomato, feta and mint.

The cake is served in surprisingly hefty portions for such a sleek and sophisticated environment: a slice of rich, moist dark chocolate cake needs more than a single cup of coffee, but it's no hardship to order another, as Black Isle serves some of the best coffee in town. A banana hazelnut loaf sits just on the enjoyable side of worthy, but the salted chocolate brownie is total indulgence. The cookies (*Kekse* in German) are equally generously proportioned and much too good to ignore, and, in any case, Black Isle Bakery lore, as set out on the whimsically worded website would have us 'Take a bun or two with tea to refresh the mind' •

Blé

Thessaloniki, Greece

📍 19 Agias Sofia
Thessaloniki
546 23, Greece
⚑ ble.com.gr

If you only have one thing here,
try the tsoureki.

Blé breaks with the traditions of many of the older and more established bakeries of Thessaloniki, and both locals and visitors like the novelty. The clue is in the name: blé is the French word for wheat, and here it signals not only a love for bread, but also the bakery's Francophile leanings. In just a few years since it opened, this modish bakery, *traiteur* and café has grown into a small chain. This is the main branch, on tourist-thronged Agias Sofia, where the many outdoor tables are a lure for sun-starved visitors.

The menu offers all manner of freshly prepared salads and simple dishes, plus of course quality bread, patisserie and ice cream to take away or eat in situ. If you look beyond the striking displays of sourdough breads and north European loaves, there is also much that is traditionally Greek to tempt as well. Blé is a dab hand at the many types of baklavas,

boureks and kateifis that have their origins in Asia Minor, but are very much a part of Thessaloniki's history too.

If you only have one thing here, try the tsoureki. This bread is most strongly associated with Greek Easter, as it is used to break the Lenten fast. Similar in some ways to a brioche, it has a shiny, soft, golden-brown crust and yellow interior, but the most distinctive thing about it is the aroma. Mahleb is a spice made from the seeds of a type of cherry tree, and together with freshly ground mastic – a plant resin – gives a beautiful fruity scent similar to that from an Italian panettone. The traditional version makes a popular gift when wrapped in a pretty napkin. But in Thessaloniki, a lily is there to be gilded, and it has become a fashion over the last decade or two to coat the tsoureki with white or dark chocolate and then decorate it with fruit.

This bread is now sold as a gift throughout the year, not just at Easter. If you have never tried tsoureki, start with the simplest version, which is a proper indulgence in itself ◦

A Blikle

Warsaw, Poland

📍 Nowy Świat 33, 00-001
Warsaw, Poland

🔖 blikle.pl

A Blikle celebrates its
150th anniversary in 2019.

A Polish institution with outlets stretching from Gdynia to Katowice, A Blikle celebrates its 150th anniversary in 2019. There are sixteen branches in Warsaw alone, including a sit-down spot in Warszawa Centralna station, a rare oasis of good taste and calm in a warren of busy corridors, and this branch, the showcase café on the city's show-off boulevard of Nowy Świat.

In each branch, on and around an etched mirror, there's the grand old name of A Blikle, the foundation date of 1869 and a portrait of the rather suave Antoni Kazimierz Blikle, complete with cravat and waxed moustache. Of Swiss heritage, and a confectioner by trade, he started work in the early 1860s at what was then Michalski and within ten years, he had taken over the premises. It was a see-and-be-seen hangout, where society met over faworki ('angel wings', thin, sugared pastries) and

coffee. Charles de Gaulle, who fought in the Battle of Warsaw in 1920, was a customer.

Today's Blikle feels traditional without being staid. Classic pastries include the rosehip jam doughnut (pączek z róża), forever linked with the Polish celebration of Fat Thursday (Tłusty Czwartek) before Lent. Other pączki are filled with elderberry jam, chocolate or Hungarian plum jam, and iced or glazed, but the sprinkle of dried orange zest on the rosehip variety is the perfect finish.

Fresh strawberries top the beza stracciatella, a meringue crafted in the bright colours of the Polish flag and freckled with chocolate chips, while at least three varieties of seasonal fruit crown the babeczka z owocami, a palm-sized tart filled with cream. The array of cakes and gateaux include leśna polana, with yoghurt mousse and forest

fruits; cheesecake with passionfruit (tort serowy z marakują), and the stylish tort royal – white and milk chocolate cream, with currant jam on a biscuit base. Match a slice of this dreamy creaminess with a cup of A Blikle's own blend of coffee – 100 per cent arabica Brazilian beans with a touch of dried fruit ⊙

Bougatsa Giannis

Thessaloniki, Greece

⚲ Mitropoleos 106,
Thessaloniki
546 21, Greece
⚑ bougatsagiannis.com

Bougatsa is a sandwich of filo pastry filled with a sweet semolina custard then sprinkled with icing sugar.

Bougatsa joints are fun, convivial, low-priced caffs that are open from the early hours of the morning. They cater for travellers disembarking from overnight ferries, drinkers trying to sober up, post-clubbers and a few early birds seeking bougatsa for breakfast. Bougatsa is a sandwich of filo pastry filled with a sweet semolina custard then sprinkled with icing sugar, and it's found in localised parts of Greece from Chania in Crete to Halkidiki. The Thessalonian versions of bougatsa take more innovative forms: fillings might include savoury elements, from mizithra cheese to minced meat. Bougatsa Giannis takes the dilemma out of which bougatsa to order, sweet or savoury, by selling a portion than is half and half – cheese on one side, sweet on the other. Accompany this with a small plastic bottle of chocolate milk from the fridge. The crisp filo pastry yields easily to the bite; the custard, cheese or mince then hits the palate. It's easy to see why it has so many devotees.

Giannis is widely considered to be the best bougatsa joint in Thessaloniki, yet it's a humble venue. The logo on the sign at the entrance shows the two curved blades used to slice the pastries at right angles. There are simple seats and tables inside, but many customers opt for take-away, or lean on the high counter outside. There is always a queue, so the bougatsa is invariably fresh, usually still warm from the oven.

The origins of bougatsa are not clear. Many Greeks maintain that the dish originates in Macedonian town of Serres, in what is now the modern state of Greece, but other theories carry equal weight. It could be Turkish – the sweet börek, laz böreği, is remarkably similar to bougatsa, and the savoury versions of this dish are everywhere in Istanbul too. Bougatsa as a word seems related to Turkish poğaça, another savoury roll sold in streets as a quick breakfast, while in Hungary you get stuffed pastries called pogacsa, and so on with variant names and dishes across the Balkans. Wherever its origins lie, bougatsa is now an emphatically Greek dish, and this is the place to eat it ⊙

Bread Ahead

London, England

♀ Borough Market,
Cathedral Street, London
SE1 9DE, England
🏃 breadahead.com

The doughnuts are a social media
sensation. They're also top notch.

A vibrant London bakery, with a mini empire of shops, cafés and baking schools, Bread Ahead is a major presence at Borough Market. Purchases made from the market stalls are made more enticing by the view of the bakers in action through the big glass windows of the bakery and baking school. The stalls look pretty good too, with a magnificent spread of doughnuts, and a wealth of bread; notably focaccias in all shapes, sizes and flavours. The doughnuts are a social media sensation. They're also top notch (Justin Gellatly, formerly head baker at St John Bakery, has worked his magic on them) and come in an enticing set of custardy, jammy flavours: vanilla, praline, caramel, raspberry jam, Eton mess, lemon meringue, honeycomb . . .

The Chelsea outpost is a more mellow experience. On a quiet street just off Sloane Square, it comprises a bakery, a café and a baking school. The interior is pared down, with decoration limited to a few copper jelly moulds and some tartan wallpaper. On our last visit, customers ranged from glossy Chelsea ladies to construction workers in hi-vis vests, and the viennoiserie display was a dream: croissants, pain au chocolat, Chelsea buns, Danish pastries and kouign-amann. The Soho branch is different again, with brightly painted walls and a homespun vibe. Bread takes a backseat here, with filled rolls, pastries (including cinnamon buns) and pretty cakes to the fore.

The baking courses are a big part of the business, and range from family-friendly two-hour slots, through half- and full-day bread and patisserie workshops, to a three-day 'Guide to Sourdough Bread' option ⊙

Bread Source

Aylsham, England

📍 13 Red Lion Street,
Aylsham, Norfolk
NR11 6ER, England
🔗 bread-source.co.uk

The densely satisfying sourdough, made from local flour, a little seasalt, water and some wild magic, is a daily bestseller.

The source of owner Steve Winter's daily bread is Horsham St Faith, a village about five miles from Norwich, where he has his own mill. This baker does nothing by halves. In his quest to create truly local loaves, he seeks out slow growing wheat from Norfolk farmers, which is delivered to his Austrian stone mill for grinding, before being set on the long, slow proving and fermenting journey to create exceptionally tasty bread. As the name suggests, provenance is all, and people who come to this winsome, whitewashed shop in the market town of Aylsham can rest assured their sourdoughs, baguettes and multigrains are at the vanguard of the slow food revolution, having taken many hours to take shape.

The densely satisfying sourdough, made from local flour, a little seasalt, water and some wild magic, is a daily bestseller, but weekend shoppers make a beeline for the granola loaf, with its sweet and sticky fruit and nut crust (coconut, hazelnut, fig and apricot all baked in) – perfect for an indulgent breakfast. Then there's the raisin brioche, that delightful halfway house between bread and cake, some glorious pastries and sweet, doughy little buns filled with redcurrants, blueberries and raspberries.

The big, light croissants are nicely round and puffy, while the almond version is huge and golden, flecked with nuts and lightly striped with chocolate.

This is the original branch, but it has recently been joined by a sleeker, city sister. Bread Source in Norwich is an airy, minimalist space on Upper St Giles Street, where the stars of the show – the loaves – are artfully displayed on special bread pegs and the price list set out on rolls of brown paper. This branch also has a pretty little courtyard garden, which makes the offer of a 'bottomless' cup of filter coffee all the more irresistible ●

Bread Station

London, England

⚲ Arch 373 Helmsley Place,
London E8 3SB, England
⚑ thebreadstation.co.uk

A winning mash-up of Danish-meets-east-London baking.

The Bread Station in the London Borough of Hackney is the result of a collaboration between two Danes, Michelin-starred chef Christoffer Hruskova and master baker Per Brun, and the end result is a winning mash-up of Danish-meets-east-London baking. As is often the London way, the bakery is housed in a railway arch; this one is just around the corner from E5 Bakehouse, and next to Climpson's coffee HQ, right in the heart of foodie Hackney.

The atmosphere is anything but po-faced though – the bright, white café feels like an extension of the bakery area (there's a thriving wholesale side to the business), and is divided from the action by a rack of breads, a carefully edited array of baked goods and a much-used coffee machine. There are tables and chairs outside in the front yard, too. There's a steady stream of customers taking away a coffee (by Caravan) and a croissant, as well as diners getting stuck into a bacon sandwich. Along the side wall are a few own-made goods (granola, muesli) and their own-milled wholemeal flour, plus a handful of products from trusted suppliers (London Borough of Jam preserves, for example). Breakfasts and big sandwiches are listed on blackboards – fillings change, but spicy beef brisket with pickles and mayo is typical – plus a few hot dishes such as shakshuka, and a selection of smørrebrød.

Loaves are 100 per cent organic, both additive- and yeast-free, and have a wonderful crust and texture. The range is reassuringly small, but encompasses rye breads (including a dark, fruity rye) and a chunky baguette, as well as mainstays such as the Hackney wholemeal, a sourdough loaf that's a mix of Wiltshire and Italian flours, both milled on site. This and the London Fields seeded are favourites for toasting. The counter holds madeleines, brownies, brioches and assorted pastries, including a variety of cinnamon buns and the Dirty Dane, a doughy, chocolate-laced treat. At weekends there are specials, such as Kringle (an apple, cinnamon and sugar sweet bread) ○

Brotgarten

Berlin, Germany

Seelingstraße 30, 14059 Berlin, Germany
brotgarten.de

This vegetarian bakery, shop and café wears its hippy origins with pride.

The pretty little streets just south of the thundering road Spandauer Damm, not far from the grandiose Schloss Charlottenburg, yield some browsable shops and cafés: the fairest of them all is Brotgarten. The first wholegrain bakery collective in the city (it opened in 1978), this vegetarian bakery, shop and café wears its hippy origins with pride – and it was producing great Sauerteig (sourdough) loaves long before the hipster joints came along. The signature loaf is the classic dark and sour rye, which has a long bread bin life and makes filling toast, and a fine match for avocado. Rye (Roggen) generally is a speciality, and the dark loaves baked with caraway, coriander, fennel or cardamom have a perfectly crusty outside and a pleasing density inside. These savoury breads are on the menu in the café next door, alongside the oft-praised vegetable soup,

or accompanying salads or cheese and pickles. Some of the big, round multi-seeded loaves are things of beauty – encrusted with a patchwork of poppy, sesame, pumpkin and other adornments – and a very welcome contribution to any feast. Loaves of spelt, wheat and mixed grain fill the wooden shelves; the bakery produces up to twenty-nine different types of bread every day, and they sell fast. Staff don't have much time to chat, so ponder the various croissants, pastries and fruit strudels in the glass-fronted counter, and have your order ready.

The shop and café are both very popular with vegans, as there's a large choice of rich, but dairy-free toasted almond shortbreads, cakes, rolls and flapjacks to go with soya or almond-milk cappuccinos. Non-vegan cakes include seasonal fruit gateaux, or the more traditional cinnamon-

spiced apple cake. The crisp, sweet wholegrain Linzertorte is a hazelnutty triumph, perfect for *Kaffee und Kuchen* time. There's not a lot of room to sit inside, but there are plenty of tables outside on the pavement. Before you go, have a wander round the excellent bakeshop/deli, where you can buy bags of intriguing freshly milled flour of various hues, in the hope of recreating your own Brotgarten wholegrain experience at home ⊙

C'an Joan de S'aigo

Palma, Spain

Calle Can Sanç 10, 07001
Palma, Mallorca, Spain

canjoandesaigo.com

Quintessentially Mallorcan treats both sweet and savoury, all made on the premises to time-honoured recipes.

Set in an alley in the historic heart of Palma, furnished with traditional tiles and marble tables and strewn with antiques (yes, that's an eighteenth-century tulipière), C'an Joan de S'aigo appears every inch a historic institution. Which is only half true. This family-run café/bakery has inhabited these premises only since the 1980s, but most of the furnishings, the larger part of the menu and all of the tradition were reverently imported from earlier incarnations of the business, founded in 1700.

C'an Joan de S'aigo's menu features quintessentially Mallorcan treats both sweet and savoury, all made on the premises to time-honoured recipes. Here are the ensaïmadas ubiquitous in Palma – spirals of lard-shortened pastry filled with custard (the classic), chocolate, candied pumpkin or peach – along with the less common cuarto, the gentle flavour and bouncy sponge texture of which only make sense if, as directed by the gravely attentive staff, you tear off chunks to dip in the intense, house-made hot chocolate. A skilled pastry maker contributes little pasty-like cocarrois, stuffed with seasonal vegetables, and meat pies that bear an uncanny resemblance in their raised crust to the British pork pie.

Perhaps the most emblematic product here is the ice cream, served in a glass and made as it was 300 years ago, when it was marketed as a medicinal product for its cooling and nutritional properties, particularly the almond version. Mallorca's almonds are known for their sweetness and high oil content (as well as turning the island's early spring landscape into a froth of pinky-white), and an order of ice cream helps support the precarious living of the farmers who cultivate them.

But surely the claim to use original production methods can only be a piece of mythologising, since refrigeration had had yet to be invented in the early 1700s? Not at all. The very origins of C'an Joan S'aigo are enshrined in the ancient Mallorcan practice of harvesting ice from stone-built enclosures which trapped wind-blown snow on the island's Serra de Tramuntana mountain range. Founder Joan de S'aigo was himself a *nevater* (ice maker), who endured punishing trips into the mountains to monetise this precious commodity. Look out for the two copper-coloured cylinders, which were used in the early ice-cream making process

Caffè Sicilia

Noto, Italy

📍 Corso Vittorio Emanuele III 125, 96017 Noto, Sicily, Italy
📞 +39 0931 835013

Traditional Sicilian pastries include hand-rolled cannoli stuffed with sweet ricotta cream.

Located in deepest south-east Sicily, the honey-hued town of Noto is famous for its glorious Baroque architecture. But for foodies, just as important as the gargoyles and the flowery flourishes is an unremarkable looking *pasticceria* set on the main drag close to the Chiesa di San Carlo. Caffè Sicilia was founded in 1892 and is the domain of the self-effacing Corrado Assenza, master gelato maker and pastry chef. It's an old-fashioned sort of a place; the bustling front bar, with its hissing coffee machine and eye-catching selection of cakes and pastries in glass cases, is usually occupied by locals propping up the counter while sipping on their umpteenth espresso of the day. The *sala* at the back, filled with small round wooden tables, is more genteel, while visitors tend to sit out front when the weather is good.

Born and bred in Noto, after a stint in Bologna studying agronomy, Assenza returned to his roots to take over his family business (he is the fourth generation) – rekindling a passion acquired as a small boy who passed hours in the kitchen with his maestro Roberto Giusto, watching, tasting and learning. He is featured in an early episode of the *Chef's Table* Netflix series of documentaries, but it's unlikely that fame will go to this modest man's head, he's still working hard in Caffè Sicilia, assisted by his son Francesco.

Evangelical in his enthusiasm about the natural bounty on his doorstep ('we have the best ingredients in the world in Sicily'), there is an element of alchemy in Assenza's icy creations, and it's appropriate that he refers to his kitchen as his *laboratorio*: the palate challenging caper and olive ice cream comes with an onion ice cream centre. As well as his incomparable ice creams, cakes and pastries, he also makes granite (simply water, sugar and a natural flavouring). He started off with a fairly traditional repertoire of recipes, but has been drawn increasingly to experimentation. His granite these days are flavoured not only with creamy Noto almonds, mandarin oranges or tart local lemons, but also strawberry and tomato, spicy basil, and even oysters paired with almonds. (Granita, by the way, is eaten for breakfast in Sicily, usually accompanied by a sweet brioche pastry; it's much too hot for cappuccino.)

Smooth ice cream is made from *gelsi* (mulberries) plucked from trees down the road, pistachios from Bronte on the slopes of Etna, chocolate from nearby Modica flavoured with candied orange peel and cinnamon and ricotta from a local sheep farmer. The sense of place is irrefutable.

Traditional Sicilian pastries and cakes made here include hand-rolled cannoli stuffed with sweet ricotta cream, pistachio-green cassatine topped with shiny white icing and a cherry, and peach and rhubarb or saffron and almond cakes. Then there are tiny almond biscuits flavoured with orange rind and hand-moulded marzipan fruits, their skins dusted with coloured powders to create a realistic, ripe blush. Not to mention the flavoured honeys, hand-made chocolates, nut-based spreads, pistachio or almond nougat . . . ◉

Café Succès

Helsinki, Finland

📍 Korkeavuorenkatu 2,
00140 Helsinki, Finland
📞 +358 9 633414

The arrival of a tray of fresh korvapuusti causes quite a stir and it's not unusual to see a line form, especially in winter.

'A slap round the ear' – it doesn't sound appealing but that's the translation of korvapuusti, one of the best buns in Helsinki. Sweet dough is rolled, folded and sprinkled with cinnamon; hot from the oven the aroma is worth the price alone. No prizes for guessing what the finished item is meant to resemble.

Nobody does korvapuusti better than snug Café Succès in Helsinki's Ullanlinna quarter. The arrival of a tray of fresh korvapuusti causes quite a stir and it's not unusual to see a line form, especially in winter, as people are drawn in by the combined wafts of cinnamon and coffee. It's not just the freshness of the buns at Café Succès; it's their sheer size. Homemade versions are a common treat in Finnish homes, but they're often a fraction of the size of these behemoths.

Also popular are equally large jam and custard buns, as well as seasonal specialties such as laskiaispulla. These are Shrove buns: a kind of giant, cream-filled burger flavoured with cardamom and dusted with icing sugar, plus a dollop of either jam or almond paste. The café is also a great place to sample Runebergin torttu, a sumptuous cylindrical cake featuring almonds and sometimes rum, topped with a raspberry jam crown contained in a ring of icing. It's served on and around 5 February to celebrate of the birthday of the nineteenth-century national poet, J.L. Runeberg.

A few pavement tables and chairs complete with blankets offer excellent people-watching vantage points; inside there are newspapers and space for laptop workers. Salad and filled fresh bread rolls appear at lunchtime. There's also a bigger, busier and less intimate branch, Café Esplanad, but compact Café Succès remains the favourite after more than six decades ๐

La Campana

Seville, Spain

⌖ Calle Sierpes 1–3, 41004 Seville, Spain
⚲ confiterialacampana.com

This traditional patisserie is right at the city's nerve centre, and its terrace is the perfect see-and-be-seen spot.

La Campana is in Seville's old town, but it's hardly tucked away down a winding alley. At the head of Calle Sierpes, the city's main shopping street, and next to busy Plaza del Duque del Victoria, this traditional patisserie is right at the city's nerve centre, and its terrace, which looks out from a tiny square, is the perfect see-and-be-seen spot. Sevillanos drop in for an ice cream or a stand-up coffee at the counter or to pick up pastries to take home.

Opened in 1885, La Campana was a supplier to royalty, and it remains a family business. Founder Antonio Hernández Merino, his wife Margarita and their eight sons invested in quality, and the splendid exterior and wood-panelled interior, both decorated with early art nouveau paintings and glasswork, remain largely unchanged. All the baked goods are still made daily, by hand and without shortcuts, though

not everything is made on the premises any more. Some of the pastries can take a full day to prepare, from start to finish, but hurrying a dough would impede the development of flavour. La Campana also turns out its own ice cream, hand-made chocolates and candied fruits (fruta escarchada).

Antique cabinets proffer Spanish and Seville versions of French/ European classics, such as delicious milhojas (mille feuilles) flavoured with Spanish nougat (turrón), palmiers, truffles and cream buns, plus the interestingly titled Inglès (English), a sticky apple confection. The more traditional offerings are more puritan and rather drier: the name of the torta de polvorón derives from *polvo*, or dust. It's a Christmas delicacy, but available here year-round. There's pretty much a cake for every religious occasion in party-loving

Catholic Seville, and La Campana makes its own Holy Week snacks (torrijas and pestiños) and particularly fine roscos de reyes at Christmas. These 'biscuits of the kings' are made to commemorate the arrival of the Magi and are traditionally eaten for breakfast on 6 January. They are decorated with gleaming candied fruit to represent the kings' jewelled garments and contain a figurine of a king (for luck) and a dried bean (for buying the next rosco).

Don't leave Seville without sampling a yema Sevillana – these Arab-influenced candied egg yolks are an acquired taste, but very much a local delicacy. Such is the city's confectionery culture that the yemas are just one of many confections commonly sold by nuns from within their cloisters (at Convento de San Leandro, for example), but also available amid the grandeur of La Campana ◦

Casa Aranda

Malaga, Spain

📍 Calle Herrería del Rey 3,
29005 Malaga, Spain
📞 +34 952 22 28 12

While the churro might appear a simple snack – merely a length of dough fried in olive oil – the process behind it is complex.

The fried sticks of dough known as churros are a traditional breakfast and teatime snack throughout Spain, and one that engenders a certain amount of competition, with each region trumpeting the supremacy of its own version. The churro tradition is probably most entrenched in Madrid, but Andalucians argue that because the dough used in their own version, whether it's tejeringo (Malaga and Granada), tallo (Jaén) or calentito (Seville), cannot be frozen, the end result is always superior.

Another reason why the Malagueno churro in particular is a benchmark of quality is that since 1932 Casa Aranda has been its standard bearer, and Casa Aranda's standards are exacting. Founder Antonio Aranda Cuenca grew up in a wheat-producing area just outside town, and he knew his flours. He spent two years in the kitchen testing samples and devising the optimum mix of flour, salt and olive oil. The same flour and the same recipe are still in use today.

While the churro might appear a simple snack – merely a length of dough fried in olive oil – the process behind it is complex. It won't do to have either the churro or the customer sitting around, so the timing has to be perfect. For speed, the dough is usually extruded directly into the pan in a single rope. In Casa Aranda's early days, this was done using a *churrera de hombro*, a giant syringe whose plunger was braced against the operator's shoulder. To hold its shape, the dough needs to be thick, so this was a man's job – Cuenca wielded the *churrera* while his sister Liliota served coffee brewed in a pan from behind the marble counter. (It should come as no surprise that when the time came to automate, perfectionist Cuenca summoned a renowned churros mechanic all the way from Ceuta, on the north coast of Africa.)

To fill the pan, the dough is directed by hand into a spiral, from the inside (regarded as a delicacy) out: this must be done quickly and precisely enough for the middle not to burn before the outer ring is cooked. It's flipped, then scissored swiftly into sticks and whisked away by a white-jacketed waiter, typically accompanied by a hot chocolate (a thick one, so as not to drip as you dip) or a coffee. Note that Malaga has a coffee terminology all of its own, so ask for a mitad rather than a con leche.

This is budget fast food, so the surroundings are about serving the customers quickly rather than encouraging them to linger. Inside, the café is furnished with a metal counter, basic furniture and paper napkins; outside you'll find zinc-topped tables and plastic chairs where you can watch the world go by – and people from all over the world do come here, along with crowds of locals. Casa Aranda is open every day, even Sundays, when the tradition is to drop by after mass, but note that the business enjoys a prolonged siesta from 12.30pm to 5pm daily ●

Chambelland

Paris, France

📍 14 rue Ternaux,
75011 Paris, France

🔖 chambelland.com

Chambelland not only produces tasty gluten-free bread but also patisseries, cakes and cookies that more than hold their own against their gluten-packed peers.

Creating a decent gluten-free loaf is quite a challenge, and it's one that many bakers have failed. So it's a pleasant surprise to find Chambelland bakery in the Oberkampf, which not only produces tasty gluten-free bread but also patisseries, cakes and cookies that more than hold their own against their gluten-packed peers.

The business was established in 2014 by Nathaniel Doboin and Thomas Teffri-Chambelland, who decided that the best way of sourcing guaranteed gluten-free flours was to have their own mill. The duo chose the Haute-Provence region of France, close to the Camargue rice growers, and today the mill produces flours from rice, buckwheat, sorghum and millet. Teffri-Chambelland, a former biochemistry teacher, applied a scientific approach to creating dough from these flours, and judging by the results, it's paid off. The bakery's line of breads not only look the

part but deliver too, with light, airy insides and a satisfyingly crunchy crust. The Chambelland rice flour loaf doesn't have the same attributes as traditional wheat bread – the texture is springy, rather than soft – but it really doesn't matter: it tastes good. Varieties, all certified organic, include five-grain bread, sourdough and focaccia.

Sweet alternatives feature a pain au chocolat (an actual chocolate loaf, not a pastry), and a delicious sweet rice flour bread, available in several flavours (a great alternative to a croissant). Even sweeter treats include a lemon meringue tart, chocolate chip cookies, coconut macaroons and the so-called 'browkie', a cross between a brownie and a cookie that is rich, melt-in-the-mouth crumbly and addictively moreish.

Customers can linger in the casual, contemporary café space or, on a sunny day, at a table outside in

the small square within which the bakery sits. A modest range of creative sandwiches made from Chambelland's own breads are available for lunch, plus seasonal soups and salads. Given the stream of customers through the door on an average weekday morning, it's clear the bakery is a success, and not just with those on a gluten-free diet ◦

Chatzis

Thessaloniki, Greece

📍 50 Venizelos Street,
Thessaloniki 546 31,
Greece

🔗 chatzis.gr

Unique to Thessaloniki is the trigona panoramatos: triangles of filo pastry soaked in syrup then piped full of a dense custard.

A framed sepia postcard on the wall of Chatzis reads 'Souvenir de Salonique, Turquie'. In the intervening century since that view of the harbour was captioned, Salonika ceased to be part of the Ottoman Empire, and the city's name was Hellenised to Thessaloniki as the Greek nation state grew. But the fact remains that Salonika was one of the great Ottoman cities, second only to Istanbul. The Turks left and the mosques and hammams fell into disrepair, but their Anatolian culinary heritage remains. And at Chatzis – established in 1908, a decade before the collapse of the Ottoman Empire – you get a full taste of those vanished days.

It's an old-fashioned bakery and café, filled with dessert-packed glass display cases, and with small tables marshalled by equally diminutive waitresses. This zaxaroplasteio (dessert shop) moved to this corner site in 1917 – the fire that destroyed most of Salonika's wooden buildings also razed the original bakery. A few older men sit at the pavement tables whiling away the time over Greek coffees. Others order from the laminated menu, which has detailed descriptions in English as well as Greek.

There are typical Greek savoury snacks, a huge array of unusual soft drinks, and scores of the syrupy sweets that were once eaten as daytime snacks, but that we now call desserts. You could start with a cup of salep, the aromatic winter drink made from a type of orchid tuber that's flavoured with cinnamon, cloves and ginger – it's like a confected hot malt drink. Or there's boza, the millennia-old Balkan drink made from fermented corn and millet; it's thick and has a mild sour-sweet flavour, plus a low alcohol content (less than 1 per cent).

This is one of the few places where you'll find ekmek kataifi (ekmek being the Turkish word for bread), a dish originating in Anatolia's opium poppy region that uses kataifi – long strands of spun wheat pastry – as a base, soaked in sugary syrup then topped with a thick custard. There are also the more usual baklavas and halvas. But unique to Thessaloniki is the trigona panoramatos: triangles of filo pastry soaked in syrup then piped full of a dense custard, like a Greek version of Sicilian cannoli ◦

Companio Bakery

Manchester, England

📍 35 Radium Street,
Manchester M4 6AD,
England

⚲ companiobakery.co.uk

The commitment to locally sourced ingredients is reflected in the names of the loaves.

Although a relative newcomer (2015) to Manchester's bakery ranks, Companio has established itself as an essential part of the Ancoats district revival. Artisan baker Russell Goodwin has built a reputation for quality goods combined with an innovative operating approach: Companio is part-funded by the community, collaborates with local suppliers and actively participates in local life. The shop is only open during the day on Tuesdays and Thursdays (Russell, who runs the place pretty much single-handedly, is trying to achieve a work-life balance), but join the Company Bread Club and you can collect the loaves from nearby Rudy's Pizza on those evenings, too. Any bread left after the shop is closed is sold by Russell at Manchester Victoria train station (4–6pm Tuesday and Thursday).

Companio makes 'real bread' – no processing aids or artificial additives – and all breads are sourdoughs. The range of loaves isn't huge, but the slow fermentation required for sourdough production gives an irresistible depth to the flavour. The commitment to locally sourced ingredients is reflected in the names of the loaves. The Salford-5-Seed (linseed, poppy, pumpkin, sesame and sunflower), the basic Northern Rose sourdough, the Pennine rye and the Victoria wholewheat all vie for the top spot over the no-nonsense Ancoats white. Try the savoury 'Danish', delicious, hearty swirls made using pizza dough, in vegetarian (cheddar, red onion, rocket and basil pesto) and non-vegetarian (bacon, rocket and tomato pesto, cheddar and red onion) choices. There's usually a couple of cakes too; on a recent visit, chocolate with almond and sherry, and Bramley apple and cinnamon were featured.

Links with the community are also fostered by bread-making and patisserie courses, held on the premises on Sundays. Whether you choose Introduction to Bread Making, Sourdough Basics or Artisan Patisserie training, you get to take home what you've made ◦

Comptoir Gourmand

London, England

📍 96 Bermondsey Street,
London SE1 3UB, England
🔗 comptoirgourmand.co.uk

The little chouquettes are a delight,
sold in tens and gone in a flash.

As the name suggests, the cakes and pastries made by London's Comptoir Gourmand have a French accent. Styles and techniques are predominately French, from the rich canelé de Bordeaux to the chocolate eclair, though a few non-French items (like the chocolate brownie) sneak through. Pastry chef Sebastien Wind started with a stall at Borough Market in 2005, and the business has now expanded to include two shops, as well as stalls at several other London markets.

The charming Bermondsey Street shop is tiny, but manages to cram in a few stools for perching on and a coffee machine, alongside a fine spread of viennoiserie (try the scrumptious fruit Danishes), a selection of filled rolls, flatbreads and toasties, and some mini quiches. The window display is almost impossible to walk past; an ever-changing array might include pasteis de nata, apple tarts, croissants and pain aux raisins. The little chouquettes are a delight, sold in tens and gone in a flash; madeleines come stuffed with salted caramel or topped with lemon icing. Patisseries include individual tarts, notably an exquisite lemon, and mille-feuille slices. Not as pretty but just as tempting is the Comptoir Gourmand version of an English sausage roll: flaky pastry wrapped around cooked onions and a whole herby sausage. Arranged behind the counter is a range of sourdough breads from local wholesaler, the Snapery. Take a Monmouth coffee and an almond croissant to the little park across the road, and you're set up for the day.

At the Druid Street site, the café (entrance on Maltby Street) is more spacious and shares a converted railway arch with the bakery. Here there's more room for savouries such as pizza slices; in colder months you might be lucky enough to coincide with their tartiflette stall, located just outside the door. Both branches are blessed with notably cheery staff ◦

ConditCouture

Frankfurt, Germany

⚲ Fahrtor 1 (Am Römerberg), 60311 Frankfurt, Germany

⚲ conditcouture.com

High-end artisan products, made by hand from scratch and presented in seasonal collections.

A charming little cake shop-cum-café tucked into the bottom corner of a gorgeous half-timber building, ConditCouture is located in Frankfurt's old town, and is a perfectly placed pit stop between museums, or on a walk from the river to the Römerberg (Frankfurt's old town square, where the city's sprawling Christmas market takes place). Yet despite being in a popular tourist spot, this tiny patisserie remains very popular with locals.

ConditCouture prides itself on its high-end artisan products, made by hand from scratch and presented in seasonal collections. The beautiful array includes modern French patisserie, as well as some German – and some uniquely Frankfurt – cake and pastry classics. Of the former, choose from yoghurt torte with passionfruit and redcurrants, and all manner of petit fours and pralines; from the latter, there's Bienenstich (beesting cake), Apfelstrudel (apple strudel) and a very good vegan Linzertorte. During carnival season, the windows are piled high with traditional Kreppel (doughnuts); Easter sees marzipan chicks and rabbits on display. Hone in on a bite-sized Frankfurter Bethmännchen ('little Bethmann') at Christmastime – a simple marzipan pastry flavoured with powdered sugar and rosewater and formed into a small ball decorated with three almonds. And at any time of year, a slice of Frankfurter Kranz is a must: ConditCouture is a rarity in still hand-making the traditional buttercream icing for this regal-looking layer cake of sponge, jam, buttercream and nut brittle.

To experience all this, however, you first have to get through the door – quite a feat, as ConditCouture is absolutely tiny. The cosy space has a glass counter, gaudy wallpaper and dangling bare lightbulbs; more often than not, the queue snakes out into the street. There's very limited seating inside: if you're lucky enough to grab a tall stool at one of the bar tables, make the most of it and stay for a cup of coffee or a hot chocolate. If not, take your pastry and enjoy it down by the river. In summer, ice cream is served from a second counter by the window and additional seating is provided on the red-brown cobbles outside ●

Conditorei Péclard im Schober

Zurich, Switzerland

⚲ Napfgasse 4, 8001
Zurich, Switzerland
⚓ peclard-zurich.ch

An exquisite example of a nineteenth-century coffeehouse in the heart of Zurich's Niederdorf district.

Péclard Schober is a bakery, chocolatier and café. It is small but perfectly formed, much like the chocolates it sells. It's a place so fascinating from the outside – the window displays, like those of nearly all the boutiques and emporiums in this part of Zurich, are beautiful – you almost forget to venture inside. However, venture inside you should.

Established in 1845 as Eberle's Süsskramladen (Eberle's sweet shop), the place was taken over by Theodor Schober in 1874. In 2009 it came under the wing of Swiss restaurateur Michel Péclard, who restored it to its former glory as an exquisite example of a nineteenth-century coffeehouse in the heart of Zurich's Niederdorf district – a well-preserved old part of town where winding cobblestone streets rise steeply to overlook the pretty, glass-green of the Limmat river.

Péclard Schober has a charming front terrace, which is a lovely spot to sit and watch the well-heeled go by. It's just off the main drag so it doesn't feel like a tourist trap, although be prepared for inner-Zurich prices. The menu is a slim yet elegant list of breakfasts of gipfeli (croissant) and other sweet buns, and lunches of quiches, sandwiches and salads. There's a good selection of coffee and teas, as well as afternoon aperitifs. It's worth sampling the decadently sweet Shoggi Mélange drinking chocolate, which is so thick you may never reach the bottom of the glass, accompanied by a slice of Gugelhupf or an Apfelstrudel. Or try the patisserie – perfect little fruit tarts and fancy slices. To take away, the delicate house-made artisanal chocolates come in pretty blocks or tempting truffles.

For those seeking more privacy, there's also a sunny, secluded side courtyard, or the neo-Baroque Salon Rouge, an elegant tea room. It's the ideal place to snatch a quiet hour to yourself or catch up with an old friend ◦

Conditori La Glace

Copenhagen, Denmark

♥ Skoubogade 3, 1158
Copenhagen, Denmark
↑ laglace.dk

There's a choice of more than twenty layer cakes, from the Karen Blixen coffee cake to the lemon mousse, raspberry and white chocolate fantasy known as the Hans Christian Andersen.

With all the hip bakeries and cafés popping up in the Danish capital, it's easy to forget that Denmark's baking traditions are centuries old. Not many examples of that heritage remain, but Conditori La Glace, which opened its elegant doors for the first time in October 1870, has not only survived but flourished.

Located in the city's historic quarter, La Glace is a favourite with drop-in customers collecting birthday cakes and buying sweet treats, and it offers the perfect pick-me-up for footsore shoppers and tourists. There's plenty of space in the stately tea salons – 120 seats spread over four rooms, plus lots of outdoor tables in warmer months. Neatly aproned waiting staff serve straightforward coffees (no fancy lattes here) alongside rather more florid cakes, beautifully displayed in glass cabinets. Everything is made from scratch, from chocolates to tiered wedding cakes.

There's a choice of more than twenty layer cakes, from the Karen Blixen coffee cake to the lemon mousse, raspberry and white chocolate fantasy known as the Hans Christian Andersen. La Glace's pastries and patisserie list starts with a simple Lyonsnitte short crust topped with crushed macarons and raspberry jam, moves through the vibrantly coloured Carl Nielsen orange buttercream creation, and finishes with mocha eclairs and choux pastries covered with rum, chocolate or orange icing. Baked tarts include Werners Valsetærte (a tribute to dancer Jens Werner), which is filled with rhubarb and vanilla and topped off with crumble and almond flakes. Nøddebo Præstetærte, a tart crammed with hazelnuts and walnuts, is popular at Christmas. Last but not least, and in keeping with its name, La Glace offers own-made ice cream cakes, shakes and scoops ○

Conditori Nordpolen

Vara, Sweden

⚲ Torggatan 14, 53431
  Vara, Sweden
⚲ nordpolen.se

Try the regional speciality,
Läckökringlan – a kind of sweet pretzel
made with puff pastry and almonds.

This classic Swedish pastry shop was founded in 1903 by two sisters, Alma and Alvida Jansson. The name means 'the North Pole' and the venture was named after the ambitious but fatal expedition in 1897, when Salomon August Andrée tried to reach the North Pole by hot air balloon. (A trial flight had landed on a field outside Vara in 1894, an exciting event at the time.) These days, Nordpolen is an old-fashioned treat, set in a green wooden building on a corner site, with friendly service and seats in the garden in the summertime. Good coffee (in pots) and cakes are served at the table; an unusual but charming detail, as Swedish cafés are usually self-service.

Everything is made from scratch, from the chocolate pralines to the wood oven-baked sourdough bread. Creative cakes, most of them sporting whipped cream, are a speciality. The most famous Swedish cake, the princess cake, is usually covered in green marzipan, but not here – Nordpolen's bakers dream up unique designs almost every day. There is huge choice of sweet things: buns, biscuits and flaky Danish pastries, through to fancy cakes such as the Leonore (elderflower mousse, meringue and chocolate pannacotta on an almond base). Make sure you try the regional speciality, Läckökringlan – a kind of sweet pretzel made with puff pastry and almonds ○

Confiserie Graff

Frankfurt, Germany

Reichsburgstraße 12, 60489 Frankfurt, Germany
+49 69 78904861

There's a strong focus on petits gateaux – small, delicate-looking layered cream mousse tartlets – of which there's a generous, seasonally changing selection.

Confiserie Graff is a seventh-generation family business that opened in 1832. Now owned and run by master confectioner Regina Graff, this traditional bakery and patisserie has been in its present site in Frankfurt's south-western Rödelheim district since 2004. Regina grew up above her parents' bakery not far from here, her mother keeping an eye on her using a security camera installed in the shop, and many of her long-term customers to this day still know her as 'the baby from the monitor over the counter'. She learned the secrets of French patisserie in Luxembourg and travelled the world as a cruise ship pastry chef before returning to Frankfurt to take over the premises beneath her parents' new home.

It's a cosy spot, frequented by loyal local customers who often come mid-afternoon for a cup of coffee and a little something from the tempting array of sweet creations under the glass-domed counters. The assortment includes tortes and tray bakes, pastries, hand-made chocolates, macarons and thirty-five different types of pralines. The Käsekuchen (cheesecake) is popular, as is the Rödelheimer Kränzchen (Graff's mini version of the much-loved Frankfurter Kranz, complete with a slug of cherry brandy). Traditional German cakes aside, there's a strong focus on petits gateaux – small, delicate-looking layered cream mousse tartlets – of which there's a generous, seasonally changing selection. Favourites include a gorgeous almond mousse with red peach, the strawberry and rhubarb one and a wintery chestnut torte. Graff also sells a small selection of German breads and bread rolls, all hand-made with love and attention and baked using Frankfurt's only wood bread oven.

A second, very modern, clean-lined branch of Graff opened in 2017 just outside the Main-Taunus-Zentrum shopping centre. In the centre of the city, you'll find Graff's breads, cakes and pastries in Frankfurt's legendary indoor market hall, the Kleinmarkthalle. In 2018, Confiserie Graff was awarded the title of best café in (the federal state of) Hessen by Germany's authoritative gourmet magazine, *Der Feinschmecker*, which described Regina's baking skills as 'virtuoso'. The award didn't come as much of a surprise to Frankfurters: here, Confiserie Graff is a long-standing institution ◦

Cookie Jar

Newcastle,
Northern Ireland

121 Main Street,
Newcastle, County Down,
Northern Ireland
BT33 0AE
+44 28 4372 2427

The story goes that old Granny Herron had a secret recipe for wheaten bread which she grew up making for friends and family.

For decades, people have been flocking to Newcastle from all parts of County Down to buy Cookie Jar's majestic wheaten bread. These days they're joined by *Game of Thrones* fans who come to the bustling seaside resort en route to the iconic Mourne mountains, where filming takes place.

The story goes that old Granny Herron had a secret recipe for wheaten bread which she grew up making for friends and family. Encouraged by appreciative relatives, she started making a few extra loaves and selling them in the family fruit and grocery store on Main Street. Word got out that her wheaten bread was good, and within a few years the fruit and vegetable business morphed into a home bakery. Fifty years later, the bread is a multi award-winner, a busy café has joined the bright bakery in Newcastle and there's an equally thriving bakery and

small coffee shop in nearby Kilkeel. The wholesale and outside catering business is growing, too. James Herron, the current owner, also recently launched Bake Your Own – a range of dried bread mixes to take home. Though it's unlikely your home bake will ever have the smooth, velvety texture of the original. Wheaten bread – also known as brown soda in parts of Ireland – can be dry, coarse and grainy: but not from Cookie Jar. Here it also has a mild sweetness, which works equally well under a chunk of salty cheese or a layer of jam.

It's rare that anyone leaves the shop with just a loaf: the other breads (including sourdough), scones, cakes and buns are equally tempting, as are familiar local favourites such as fruit slim scones, iced finger rolls and Belfast baps ●

Cottonrake Bakery

Glasgow, Scotland

♀ 497 Great Western
Road, Glasgow G12 8HL,
Scotland

♠ cottonrake.com

The sourdough bread is baked fresh
daily and quickly snapped up.

Glasgow's longest street is home to what must be a contender for its smallest bakery/café (count yourself blessed if you snag a seat). But what Cottonrake lacks in space, it more than makes up for in quality. The choice of bread, cakes and savouries is huge, and much of the available space is taken up with displaying the wares. In fair weather, it's best to grab a take-away and eat it in nearby Kelvingrove Park or the Botanics.

Like many places that pride themselves on that magic combination of artisanal coffee and sourdough, Cottonrake has a stylish, Instagrammable look to it, with a cute, distressed wooden counter and bench seating and dark wood display shelves. The coffee is by Dear Green, a roastery in Glasgow's East End; the sourdough bread is baked fresh daily and quickly snapped up. Breakfast goods – huge, buttery croissants, fabulous cinnamon swirls and Danish pastries – don't hang around long either. Come lunchtime, the staff are preparing bruschetta and filling baguettes and rolls with the likes of salami, pastrami and attendant salad items.

The cakes deserve a special mention. The jury's still out on whether the glorious, gooey-centred treacle and pecan sponge tart, with its crisp and buttery pastry base, tops the heavenly white chocolate and raspberry one, in which the rich pale ganache goes beautifully with the slightly sharp raspberry jam (made in-house). Just don't expect a doughnut: the closest you'll get is the pink neon 'Donut Repair' sign created by David Shrigley – Cottonrake's nod to Glasgow's arty heart ◦

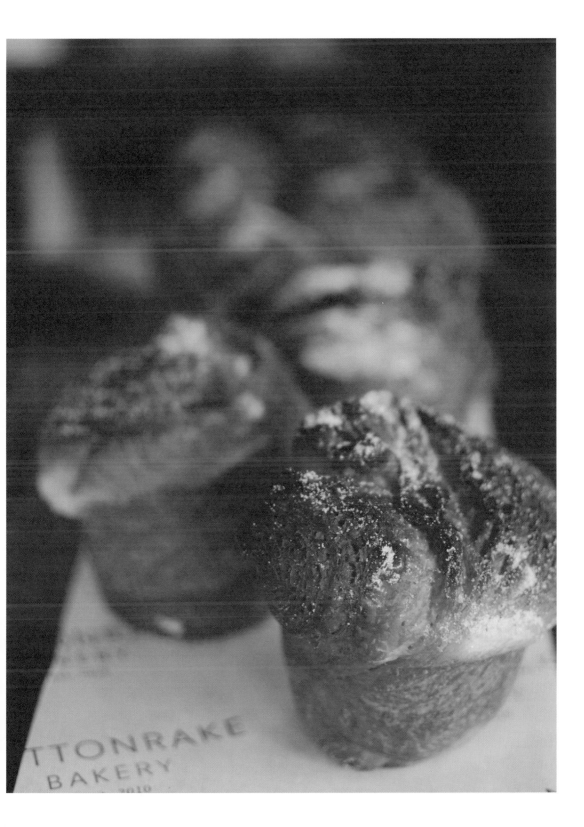

Cukrárna Myšák

Prague, Czech Republic

♀ Vodičkova 710/31, 110 00
Prague 1, Czech Republic
⚑ mysak.ambi.cz

Part of the urban fabric of Prague since 1904.

On a tram-lined street at a right angle to Wenceslas Square, Cukrárna Myšák has been part of the urban fabric of Prague since 1904, when František Myšák opened his eponymous cake shop. The renowned architects Josef Gočár and Pavel Janák, pioneers of Czech Cubism, had a hand in its singular design; regulars included famous actors, sports stars and Tomáš Masaryk, the first president of Czechoslovakia. There were often queues outside the door for Myšák's famed caramel dessert, karamelový pohár.

After surviving war and nationalisation, Myšák eventually folded in 2006, its once magnificent building a crumbling ruin. The location, though, was still referred to as 'Myšák', and in 2008, it was reborn. The interior was reconstructed from photographs, the original marble renovated and swirling-patterned wallpaper and a crystal chandelier was installed. The café once again boasted the classic cakes, flans and sundaes of yesteryear, most notably Macharův dort, a traditional chocolate favourite. In 2017, it was taken over by the Ambiente group, also responsible for the revival of the equally venerable (and ornate) Café Savoy.

The Mysák menu now includes breakfasts, fancy teas and coffees, and Central European wine. Most importantly, Karla Kahounová – who earned her spurs at the Savoy's cake counter and who now oversees the confectionery here – has given the recipes a revamp. While the Macharův dort remains sacrosanct, the Mysák sundae now has a contemporary edge, with crushed nuts in caramel complementing vanilla ice cream, coffee caramel and whipped cream. Větrník, the Czech variation of the profiterole, here has a slightly salty edge to its caramel topping. The original Myšák recipes were never written down, so Kahounová had to do some serious research, including quizzing older regulars for their memories. For them, seeing familiar names such as apple strudel with vanilla sauce (jablečný závin s vanilkovou omáčkou) and fruit dumplings (kynutý knedlík s ovocem) on the menu is reassurance that the Mysák is back on track ⊙

Damniczki

Budapest, Hungary

Hercegprímás utca 17,
1051 Budapest, Hungary
damniczkibudapest.hu

A display of eye-catching confectionery includes Williams pear pannacotta, salted peanut mousse, and blackberry and strawberry slice.

Master confectioner Balázs Damniczki learned the trade from his grandmother. He opened his first business in Székesfehérvár, near Lake Balaton, back in the 1990s, and this Budapest branch in 2016. It's an urbane café situated in the heart of the banking quarter, decorated with artist's impressions of the city's landmarks, with a popular pavement terrace. Damniczki has always gone for authenticity over easy *forints*: fresh fruit piled in, additives left out. You can taste this considered approach in creations such as blackcurrant and raspberry mousse with pistachio – it's set on a crunchy chocolate Linzer biscuit base, encircled by blackcurrant juice and offset by a scattering of pistachio and raspberry seeds.

Until mid-morning, coffee and pre-work pastries (supplied by Budapest's award-winning Mill Bakery) dominate, but once drinks and buns have flown out the door in office-bound haste, Damniczki can concentrate on his speciality. A display of eye-catching confectionery includes Williams pear pannacotta, salted peanut mousse, and blackberry and strawberry slice, of which several are available in flour- and sugar-free versions. The more gateau-like creations include 'reinvented Rákóczi cake', a contemporary reworking of the curd cheese favourite first assembled by former Gellért Hotel patissier János Rákóczi in the 1920s. As Damniczki puts it, 'This Rákóczi doesn't stick with tradition: the foam topping is much thinner, the layer of cheese thicker than usual, and the sponge light as a whisper, happy just to play a supporting role.' He also puts twenty-first-century touches into the Somlói Revolution, a recent Hungarian Cake of the Year winner and a masterpiece involving Belgian Callebeaut chocolate, nuts and orange zest.

At the height of summer, a range of knockout ice creams banishes the cakes to a standalone cabinet by the staircase. No one complains, as these ices are something special – fifty-two flavours in exotic combinations (red wine with raspberry, ginger malt) – and, like the patisseries, made back in Székesfehérvár, an hour's drive away o

Demel

Vienna, Austria

⚲ Kohlmarkt 14,
   A-1010 Vienna, Austria
⚑ demel.com

The window displays are an attraction in their own right: always inventive, and positively magical on festive occasions such as Easter and Christmas.

A *konditorei* (patisserie) with a long and impressive past, Demel stands on one of Vienna's smartest streets, just yards from the imposing Imperial Palace. The firm is very proud of its royal warrant (the 'K.u.K. Hofzuckerbäcker' under the name indicates that the business supplied the imperial family) – its heritage stretches back to 1786. Even though the business is no longer a family firm and the Austro-Hungarian empire is long gone, a slice of Demel's Sachertorte still seems like a sliver of living history.

The window displays are an attraction in their own right: always inventive, and positively magical on festive occasions such as Easter and Christmas, this is cake as art. These show-stopping arrangements do an excellent job of luring customers in. There's always a crush of people near the entrance, either heading towards the exquisite, mirrored shop for beautifully packaged cakes, chocolates and candied sweets, or making a beeline for the counter to examine the array of sweet baked goods. Once past this melée, through the bar, the café opens out into a series of gracious salons, patrolled by smartly uniformed waitresses and, on the ground floor, an open bakery where the curious can watch the tortes, strudels and biscuits being made. The bakers have more than sixty cake recipes at their fingertips and the selection changes daily, but the mighty Sachertorte (the much-loved, much-debated Viennese chocolate cake) and the delicate apple strudel are always available. There might be Punschkrapfen (another Viennese speciality), a rum-soaked fondant fancy, or Fächertorte, a cake stuffed with poppy seeds, walnuts, apple and plum jam, with a dollop of whipped cream as a popular accompaniment.

Savoury dishes (sausages, schnitzel) are available, but on cold winter afternoons, there's really nothing better than the Kaiserschmarren, a heart-warming concoction of light, fluffy pancake pieces with raisins and plum compote. The drinking chocolate has a lot of fans, too ●

Det Rene Brød

Copenhagen, Denmark

⚲ Rosenvængets Alle
17, 2100 Copenhagen,
Denmark
⚲ detrenebroed.dk

'We've been in business for more than thirty years,' says Hessellund. 'When we started up we were a collective of friends, baking organic bread sustainably with sourdough and long resting times.'

The bakery-café on Rosenvængets Alle, a quiet backstreet in the Østerbro district of Copenhagen, is the pick of six bearing the Det Rene Brød (Pure Bread) name. Stocked with a great selection of organic breads and pastries, it fits right in to the city's burgeoning bakery scene. However, the business, piloted by co-owner Johannes Hessellund, pre-dates the new wave of bakers.

'We've been in business for more than thirty years,' says Hessellund. 'When we started up we were a collective of friends, baking organic bread sustainably with sourdough and long resting times and everything was quite different from what "normal" bakeries had to offer at the time. What we were doing was special because of that.'

'Being local and feeling part of the local community is what we aim for,' continues Hessellund. 'Bakeries are a Danish tradition and as a rule people did not travel from place to place to visit the latest bakers, like they often do now. In spite of the trend for bread, there are actually fewer bakeries than there used to be and people are going a bit further to get good bread. For me, it is still vital to a bakery that the local community enjoys and appreciates it. It's the basis of our business, to make it cosy, to come to relax, to take a break from daily business for fifteen to twenty minutes.'

In this, Det Rene Brød has succeeded. This branch typifies the chain's neighbourhood bakery/café vibe, and has a bunch of loyal customers, many who linger at the window seats with a morning roll and coffee, or who turn up later in the day for a sandwich. Even without the charming atmosphere, the quality of the baking would draw them in. Four out of the six shops, including this one, bake their bread on site every day, including weekends. From a wide range of breads (including non-Danish items, like bagels and focaccia), the rye bread loaves are an evergreen favourite. There are scones and muffins, fruit tarts and marzipan cakes, but it's hard to beat the traditional pastries, such as tebirkes sprinkled with poppy seeds, and the cinnamon-flavoured 'snails' ◦

Dominique Ansel

London, England

♀ 17-21 Elizabeth Street,
London SW1W 9RP,
England

♠ dominiqueansel
london.com

Peer over the cake counter into
the open kitchen and you might see
giant s'mores being singed to order.

The New York Cronut king's only European outlet is a bright modern patisserie with a jaunty yellow awning, handily placed for Victoria coach station. Smiling staff add warmth to the slick, white premises, while the sweet and savoury baked goods add pops of colour. Dominique Ansel is a fêted celebrity chef, and this is a showcase for his style of fun, inventive baking. The trademarked Cronut frequently sells out by late morning – that's 350 of the croissant-doughnut hybrids shifted in just a few hours. Flavours change on a monthly basis, increasing their desirability – the Mirabelle plum and lychee variety, star of June 2018, came filled with homemade Mirabelle plum jam and topped with lychee ganache and lemon sugar.

If you fail to snag a Cronut, there are croissants, including a (not so) spicy chorizo version, pain au chocolat and kouign amann. Peer over the cake counter into the open kitchen and you might see giant s'mores being singed to order (other made-to-order options include madeleines and a dosa-style mille feuille). Pretty temptations in the glass display cabinet include tarts, cakes, eclairs, cheesecake and Ansel's take on the Paris Brest, the Paris London, featuring Earl Grey mousse, lemon curd and blackberry ganache. To go with the patisserie, there's coffee from the Gentlemen Baristas (Deerstalker blend). There are window stools for eat-and-run purchases and a small café (with outdoor space) where a smart afternoon tea menu is served Thursday to Sunday. Avocado on sourdough toast or turkey croque monsieur are typical of the savoury options – but most visitors are here for the photogenic sweet stuff ₀

Du Pain et des Idées

Paris, France

34 rue Yves Toudic, 75010 Paris, France

dupainetdesidees.com

It's easy to see why this antique boulangerie is such a hit with Japanese and English Instagrammers.

The bakery's picturesque corner site is painted an alluring blue that matches their distinctive paper bags. The interior is also lovely, its walls lined with marble and old wooden and glass counters – so it's easy to see why this antique boulangerie is such a hit with Japanese and English Instagrammers. But Du Pain et des Idées is so much more than a pretty face. It's been a bakery since 1889, and the current incarnation opened in 2002, under the stewardship of Christophe Vasseur; he once worked in the fashion trade, but gave it all up to make beautiful bread.

Sacks of flour piled up against the wall underline that this is a working bakery, producing various 'snails' (swirls of pastry with different flavours, most famously pistachio and chocolate), niflettes (little pastry tarts with custard cream), sacristan (a puff pastry twist) and chausson à la pomme, here made with fresh apple. The croissants are up there with the best in Paris. They have a glazed, crisp-ish top and are slightly weightier than some (in a good way). Du Pain et des Idées is also known for its giant slabs of pain des amis, which can be bought in small amounts – it's fabulous, flavoursome bread to toast. Also worth ordering are the mini-pavés, little breads packed with savoury ingredients.

Besides the quality of the baked goods, another big plus is that the staff are nice, and won't rush you through your order. You can extend your visit at the few benches and wooden tables available for pavement snacking (simple coffee is available alongside the pastries), but Du Pain et des Idées is much more shop than café. Don't get caught out – the bakery is open Monday to Friday only ◦

82 | EUROPE'S BEST BAKERIES

Dusty Knuckle Bakery

London, England

⚲ Abbot Street car park, London E8 3DP, England
⚲ thedustyknuckle.com

Eat in, surrounded by sacks of flour and with a view into the bakery, or soak up the sun in the rough and ready yard.

Hidden away down an unpromising-looking back street in Dalston, Dusty Knuckle rewards adventurous bread-hounds with a welcoming atmosphere, a mellow soundtrack and plenty of good things to eat. The bakery started life in a forty-foot shipping container, then graduated to this converted industrial space, which doubles as a café. Jolly staff are happy to talk through the day's lunch items; the soup is always worth ordering, and options such as leek, potato and smoked haddock come in big servings. There are salads, and inventive, giant toasties and sandwiches: chimichurri-marinated onglet steak with sweet and sour onions wedged between focaccia is typical. The baked savouries are tempting, too, from the chunky sausage roll to the vegetarian börek, a ricotta and green leaf-stuffed pastry inspired by the local Turkish community. There

might be a tart – say wild garlic, shallot, parmesan and rocket – and there's always a bacon sandwich.

There are own-made soft drinks, and good coffee from Ozone. Match this with a brioche (fruit or chocolate), croissant, pain au chocolate or apple turnover, and you're good to go. The mighty sticky bun is a little on the bready side, but comes generously threaded with raisins and cinnamon syrup. Eat in, surrounded by sacks of flour and with a view into the bakery, or soak up the sun in the rough and ready yard.

The choice of loaves runs from a straightforward sourdough to a 100 per cent rye, made using stone-milled, organic St Oates flour. The seeded rye (made with fermented, whole cracked rye and packed with all manner of seeds) is wonderful, but for something lighter, opt for the white potato sour, which they describe as 'a bit like a crumpet, with

a crispy crust'. Most of the breads have a pretty crispy crust, in truth, and if you like their style, you can sign up for one of their breadmaking sessions.

Dusty Knuckle supplies other cafés and restaurants, and is also a social enterprise, offering training and employment to disadvantaged young people, as well as running baking classes in schools and youth clubs. This has been part of the ethos from the start, when friends Max Tobias and Rebecca Oliver got together to open the bakery in 2014 ๏

e5 Bakehouse

London, England

◆ Arch 395, Mentmore
Terrace, London E8 3PH,
England
⚑ e5bakehouse.com

Deliciously moist walnut rugbrød uses soaked rye berries mixed with walnuts and linseeds.

What started as one man's (Ben Mackinnon) passion project has grown into one of the most respected artisan bakeries in London, complete with a grocery shop and a café. The whole e5 Bakehouse operation, including the electric ovens and a stone mill, is housed in a set of atmospheric railway arches close to London Fields station in Hackney. Sourdough rules here, as do organic principles. The signature Hackney Wild loaf uses a blend of heritage and modern white wheat and rye flour (all organic, grown and milled in the UK), plus water and salt. Other popular loaves are the baguette, the spelt loaf and a couple of rye bread variations – the deliciously moist walnut rugbrød uses soaked rye berries mixed with walnuts and linseeds. Other baked goods are the currant bun – gloriously chewy and only slightly sweet – and a changing roster of tarts, cakes and brownies, temptingly laid out next to the till. Chocolate cookies sit next to cinnamon buns, coconut macaroons and slices of lemon drizzle cake and, like the loaves, when they're gone, they're gone. Everything is freshly made from scratch, and by the end of the day the shelves are usually bare.

The café, tucked in and around the bakery, embodies the same commitment to organic and, where possible, local ingredients. Coffee is a big deal – the barista is kept busy – and the short menu runs from breakfast through to light lunches and savoury snacks. On Sundays there are also sourdough pizzas, baked in a wood-fired oven.

The Millhouse shop, next door to the bakery, sells e5 stone-ground flour, house roasted coffee, and own-made granola and jams, alongside goods from like-minded producers (the range goes from fruit and vegetables to ice cream and beer). The coffee beans are roasted over in Poplar, at e5 Roasthouse café. Launched in 2017, the café serves Mediterranean food and operates as part of the bakehouse's JustBread training scheme for refugees.

Keen customers can get behind the scenes and into the kitchen by taking one of the classes in sourdough breadmaking (beginner or advanced), not to mention sessions on jams and pickles, pizza, flatbreads and mezze, and general cookery ◦

Earth's Crust

Castle Douglas, Scotland

9 36-38 St Andrews Street,
Castle Douglas DG7 1EN,
Scotland

↟ earthscrustbakery.co.uk

The plaudits now come thick
and fast, including a Scottish
Bakery of the Year prize.

Earth's Crust is an award-winning bakery run by Tom van Rooyen and his Czech wife Pavlina. Tom's childhood on a Dumfries and Galloway smallholding and a wealth of culinary experience gleaned from travelling, and baking, all over the world, turned out to be the perfect proving oven for the business. The couple started it in 2011 and, at first, all the action took place in their converted garage premises in Laurieston, which had no shopfront. They would sell the loaves at local farmers' markets and to other outlets and developed a name for themselves with an earthy, crusty sourdough.

In his years as a chef, Tom had prepared food for people with various health conditions, and was inspired by the superior digestive benefits of sourdough. The long-fermented rye loaves were in huge demand, and the dark, sour borodinsky – a Russian combination of rye malt and wheat flour, water, molasses and a subtle hint of coriander – flew off the market stalls too.

Then disaster struck: a fire destroyed the bakery. The sourdough starter was all but lost, but fortunately Tom's friend Ben had been given some for his own use, so was able to repay the favour. They spent a year regrouping before finally opening up the current shop and café in Castle Douglas in July 2016. Just a year later it was named as one of the three best producers in the country in the BBC's Food and Farming awards. The plaudits now come thick and fast, including a Scottish Bakery of the Year prize at the Scottish Independent Retail Awards 2018. All this attention has been incredibly gratifying for the van Rooyens, who believe the quality of the local produce has made the bakery such a success. Sausage rolls are made with 'our own pastry recipe and locally sourced meat', and they are proud to use the fruit harvest from neighbours' gardens. A glut of rhubarb, for example, finds its way into wicked patisserie or wholesome streusels. The café is a popular lunch spot: people come a long way for the quiches, with the smoked haddock, feta and leek variety a real favourite ◦

Ekberg

Helsinki, Finland

📍 Bulevardi 9, 00120
Helsinki, Finland
⚓ ekberg.fi

On warm summer afternoons the pavement terrace is filled with coffee drinkers, served by elegant apron-clad, bow tie-wearing waitresses.

Finland's oldest bakery, Ekberg has been going since 1852, but moved to its current location in 1915. It's perfectly positioned on Helsinki's leafy Bulevardi; on warm summer afternoons the pavement terrace is filled with coffee drinkers, served by elegant apron-clad, bow tie-wearing waitresses. The *fin de siècle* style and ambience of the café, and the adjacent bakery and patisserie, have survived renovation and modernisation over the last century, and the bread and cakes are as sought after as ever.

Everything is made in house: from early morning the shelves are lined with bread, rolls and buns, with styles running from baguettes to dark rye breads. The first customers are workers jumping off at the nearby tram stop, tempted in by the alluring aromas. The choice of sugary treats runs from macarons via fruit tarts to the Napoleon cake (similar to a mille feuille), part of the cake repertoire since the beginning of the business. Seasonal specialities feature too, notably Shrove Tuesday buns spiced up with jam or almond paste, and the scrumptious Runebergin torttu (Runeberg torte), served in honour of the national poet's birthday.

A recent innovation is the deli counter. The more conservative customers protested at first, but it has been a hit with locals seeking a quick take-out lunch. Fruit and nut muesli, generously seeded crispbread, pies and quiches have also been introduced, along with breadcrumbs made from their own baguettes ○

Fabrica Das Verdadeiras Queijadas Da Sapa

📍 Volta Duche 12, 2710-630 Sintra, Portugal
📞 +351 21 923 0493

Queijadas are the signature dish, and one of the oldest of Portuguese cakes.

Sintra, Portugal

On the road between Sintra's busy train station and the town's main attractions sits this charming little tea room on the edge of a precipice. Although established in 1756, the interior feels mid-twentieth century with its bentwood chairs, small round tables and vintage-style crockery.

There's an impressive array of baked goods displayed behind the glass counter, both savoury and sweet, and nearly all of them deeply traditional.

Queijadas are the signature dish, and one of the oldest of Portuguese cakes: a simple crust filled with a cheesecake-style mixture of requeijão (a ricotta-like cheese), egg yolks and sugar, baked until lightly caramelised on top. They are far richer than most cheesecakes, and the caramelised surface gives a greater depth of flavours. They are sold by the half dozen to take away, wrapped up like a log in pretty typographically illustrated paper – a

common sight around Sintra. But if you're eating in – and you should – you can accompany yours with a choice of good teas, or a variety of coffees, such as the milky galão. English-speaking staff happily guide visitors through a score of less familiar hot drinks on the Portuguese menu.

Other sweet confections include pasteis de nata; travesseiros – which means 'pillows', made from a kind of puff pastry that's sprinkled with icing sugar and filled with a sweet cream – and delicias de leite, which are unusual and thrilling little cakes baked from sugar, milk and butter, flavoured with lemon zest. Little savoury tarts are artfully folded and decorated so prettily it seems a shame to bite into them.

The real charm of this place, though, is the atmosphere of a gentler, less hurried age, as the waitresses have time to chat and offer you teapot refills. The seat by the small window offers a dramatic view of the deep valley beyond ○

Falko

Haddington, Scotland

⦿ 91 High Street,
Haddington, East Lothian
EH41 3ET, Scotland
⬧ falko.co.uk

The rye sourdough starter, fed daily and named Heinrich, is over 100 years old.

His official title of 'Konditormeister' translates as the highest qualification for a pastry chef in Germany; the country's rigorous regulations for food and drink production mean that only a top-shelf baker with the requisite experience and exam results can claim the title. Falko's *Meisterprüfung* (masters' examination) was influenced by his adopted home in Scotland – check his website for pictures of a metre tall Baumkuchen (or 'tree cake') topped with a sugar crown, inspired by Edinburgh's gothic monument to Sir Walter Scott.

All of which might make this sound like a rather forbidding sort of place, but this couldn't be further from the truth. The premises in the historic market town of Haddington do have a certain well-heeled elegance – cream walls with sections of exposed stonework, dark wooden tabletops on wrought iron legs – but there's a bustling, welcoming kitchen, and there are just as many people queuing for homemade rolls, cakes and ice cream to take away as there are sit-in diners.

Falko's breads have a strong reputation – the rye sourdough starter, fed daily and named Heinrich, is over 100 years old – so the open sandwiches are a good place to start. The Swiss toast is topped with ham, grilled emmental and tomato, while the smoked salmon sandwich builds cucumber, cream cheese and fish on a firm rye foundation. The menu also features German specialities such as Schnitzel, Maultasche (a sort of doughy ravioli) and Käsespätzle (cheesy noodles), though you'll have to be quick at weekends as they sell out.

It's hard to choose from the array of cakes, so it's best to take your cue from the weather: a cold day suggests a warm apple strudel, dusted with powdered sugar, while sunnier occasions call for one of several gateaux or tarts, including the speciality Swabian apple tart (which hails from Falko's native region and includes a delicious vanilla cream custard among its ingredients). If you have room, the chocolate and raspberry cheesecake is also a must-try, with the traditional biscuit base swapped out for a rich, chewy brownie-like concoction ⦿

Farinoman

Aix-en-Provence, France

⚐ 5 rue Mignet, 13100 Aix-en-Provence, France

⚲ farinomanfou.fr

Ingredients used in the loaves include buckwheat, rye, kamut, spelt, chestnut, maize and various types of wheat flour, along with lots of seeds, wholegrains, spices and dried fruit.

The website of the Farinoman Fou ('mad flour man'), aka Benoît Fradette, is styled as a 'panifesto', but it's not so much a list of demands as a prose poem about personal discovery, ending with an invitation to the reader to travel with him in his voyage through baking. 'I don't just want to talk about bread, I want to put it in your mouth, and nourish life,' he writes.

Farinoman is very much boulangerie rather than patisserie; there are a few sweet items, such as cookies and flavoured brioches, but it really is all about the bread. The staples of the range, wholewheat sourdoughs both plain and flavoured – olives, sheep's cheese and creamed garlic all feature – are baked fresh Tuesday to Saturday, while more esoteric varieties such as an African-influenced wheat and millet loaf may be prepared only once a fortnight.

There are thirty varieties in total, representing the pre-industrial history of bread, and with it, humanity. Ingredients used in the loaves include buckwheat, rye, kamut, spelt, chestnut, maize and various types of wheat flour, along with lots of seeds, wholegrains, spices and dried fruit. Each has been carefully developed to have its own distinctive identity in terms of shape, texture, colour, crumb, crust and, of course, flavour. The Double Alpha, Triple Omega, for example (baked on Wednesday, also available Thursday), made with spelt and wheat flour and two kinds of linseed, is an oval loaf with an open texture, irregular air bubbles that speak to its hand-made origins, a smooth, even flavour and a thick caramelised crust with a perfect breaking point. The gluten-free multigrain is a dense cube whose section reveals closely packed almonds, rice flakes, linseeds and chia seeds and whose crust barely resists the knife. Both are delicious, and testament to the intellectual passion of this gifted baker.

The shop itself is no-frills: you can't get a coffee, and even if you could, there's nowhere to drink it. The design is all about functionality, and is far more workshop than boutique. To the right of the counter is the oven – a custom-made electric job with specially commissioned misters to aid crust formation – and to the left is the scale for weighing and pricing your bread, as is the practice in France (where it's normal just to buy a piece of a loaf) ⦿

Fazer Café

Helsinki, Finland

📍 Kluuvikatu 3, 00100
Helsinki, Finland
🔗 fazer.fi/fazercafe

Company founder, Karl Fazer, opened his French-Viennese café in 1891 when all things French were very much in vogue.

Domestically at least, Fazer is one of Finland's best-known brands, with a logo familiar to chocolate and candy lovers as well as grocery shoppers choosing bread, cakes and confectioneries in supermarkets. It's also a popular chain of cafés, and that's actually where the Fazer story has its genesis.

It all started here, on the site of the Fazer Café in central Helsinki. This is where the company founder, Karl Fazer, opened his French-Viennese café in 1891 when all things French were very much in vogue. The opening advertisement promised cakes, tea bread and ice cream, not to mention dances and wedding buffets.

The magnificent burnished steel art deco sign at the entrance is an impressive welcome, and the dome-like ceiling makes for a handsome setting. These days the furniture is much more Nordic sleek and classically modern than it was originally, but a bright and welcoming ambience remains. It's always been a popular social and business meeting place, and a handy spot for tired shoppers loaded with purchases from Esplanade and Aleksanterinkatu streets and the Kluuvi and Galleria Espland malls. Breakfasters have a choice of freshly baked croissants and rolls, and the café also serves good soup and salad lunches.

Above all though, the Fazer Café is renowned for its cakes: their colour and flamboyance dates back to the showmanship and perfectionism of the founder, who always wanted to exceed customers' expectations. There are chocolate cakes topped with fruit, strawberry and cream creations encased in marzipan, fruit and berry flans and all kinds of smaller tarts and confections. For celebratory cakes of any kind, the cake counter at the Fazer Café is the place to go ●

Flint Owl Bakery

Lewes, England

📍 209 High Street, Lewes
BN7 2DL, England

🖝 flintowlbakery.com

Sourdough comes in many guises: white, wholemeal brown, seeded or rye, or in a fig and walnut version.

As town centres go, Lewes is near perfect, with handsome, historic streets and a good number of thriving food shops. Lewes also has a strong independent streak, and Flint Owl Bakery is a perfect fit. The back to basics philosophy at the heart of the bakery means bread that's made using stone-ground, organic flour, water and salt, little or no yeast and a long fermentation period. Even the water comes from the Glynde spring, near the bakery. The bread is delivered to a batch of local businesses and sold at a number of farmers' markets, but the full range, including cakes, is available from the Flint Owl Bakery premises on Lewes High Street.

The design of the shop and café is elegant and unfussy, allowing the prettily shelved baked goodies to take centre stage. In the morning, there are croissants (plain, almond, cheese and tomato), pastries and doughnuts to enjoy alongside a Square Mile coffee made on the trusty La Marzocco machine.

Postcard Teas are a fine match for the stunningly pretty cakes and tarts, which run from the big and blowsy white chocolate and blackcurrant cake to the small and sleek dark chocolate and praline pavé. One of Flint Owl's strengths is the bakery's inventiveness: fig, almond and marmalade tart, for example, or salted caramel bundt. There's also a cream egg cupcake for Easter and a range of Christmas fillings for the doughnuts.

Less decorative but equally addictive are the breads. Sourdough comes in many guises: white, wholemeal brown, seeded or rye, or in a fig and walnut version. There are white and brown bloomers and baguettes. The café also serves breakfasts (including croque monsieur) and lunches (salads, soups, quiches). There aren't many seats, however, but if you're lucky, the sun will shine, and you can make use of the lovely walled yard out back ◦

Il Fornaio di Domenica Ordine

Turin, Italy

📍Via San Massimo 49,
Turin 10123, Italy
📞+39 011 884667

Grissinifici – bakers specialising in breadsticks – are a *Torinese* speciality, and Il Fornaio di Domenica Ordine is one of the best.

Baskets of Italy's famous grissini – dried breadsticks – appear before a meal on just about every restaurant table in the country but, in fact, these appetite-whetting morsels were originally invented in seventeenth-century Turin. The young Duke Vittorio Amedeo II of Savoy, so the story goes, had a delicate digestion, so the royal Savoy family's baker, Antonio Brunero, came up with the idea of stretching and baking dough from a local ghersa (an elongated, rather doughy wheat loaf) into long, thin, crispy, easily digestible sticks. The tale may be apocryphal – records of grissini-like foodstuffs date from even earlier – but it could explain why grissini have come to be associated with easing the digestion before a meal.

Grissinifici – bakers specialising in breadsticks – are a *Torinese* speciality, and Il Fornaio di Domenica Ordine is one of the best. The little shop looks like a traditional wooden farmstead, albeit one dominated by brown paper packs of grissini (all with transparent 'windows' so customers can view the product), peeping from drawers and dressers and even stacked on chairs. Il Fornaio is run by Domenica and her daughter, Selene, who produce breadsticks to match every preference. The sticks can be light, mid-brown or dark – the grissini equivalent of 'rare, medium, well done' – and can be made with water

(these emerge from the oven ultra-light and crispy and last longer) or olive oil (for a slightly richer taste). Flavours vary from plain to fresh rosemary to caramelised chocolate. Domenica selects her flour (white wheat 00 from a local mill) and yeasts (of which she uses a bare minimum) extremely carefully – but the secret of the artisanal grissino lies in the rolling, stretching and folding, and Domenica and her daughter are absolute masters of the art ●

La Fougasse d'Uzès

Uzès, France

📍 10 rue Jacques d'Uzès,
30700 Uzès, France
📞 +33 4 66 22 10 57

The dough is made from white flour, yeast and olive oil, and is typically formed into an oval with diagonal slits.

Fougasse is the present-day South of France incarnation of the panis focacius, a flat bread baked on a hearth (*focus*) that spread around the Roman Empire. Its progency also includes Italian focaccia. The dough is made from white flour, yeast and olive oil, and is typically formed into an oval with diagonal slits that are shaped during the rise so the final loaf resembles a giant ear of wheat. Fougasse is served in small, salty slices to accompany an aperitif or, beefed up by the addition of extra ingredients (often local produce: here in the Languedoc, lardons and pork scratchings; in nearby Provence, olives and anchovies) and accompanied by a salad, as a main course. It makes a versatile blank canvas on which the imagination of the baker can run sweet or savoury riot.

Pretty, pink-fronted La Fougasse d'Uzès wins hearts for its delicious fare, its warm, welcoming staff and its fair prices. You can watch the bakers at work in the open kitchen at the back, and on top of the wooden cabinets lining the shop floor, trays of fougasse fresh from the oven are laid out for your browsing pleasure, whole and in individual portions. Varieties might include gruyère, roquefort, pork crackling, olive, anchovy or sun-dried tomato, in bread dough or puff pastry. You can buy to take out or to enjoy at the pavement tables at the front.

Delicious though the fougasse is, the rest of the produce also competes with the best, particularly the crusty artisan bread and pastries (notably the raved-about raspberry tart). It also sells toothsome viennoiserie displayed on a quirky wall unit in the shape of a giant fougasse. Most of the produce is also available at a stall in Uzès' central market, which curls along the alleyways around Place du Marché aux Herbes on Wednesday and Saturday mornings.

To sample the classic sweet fougasse of Provence, related to brioche and similarly scented with orange flower water, you will need to take a trip south to Aigues-Mortes and visit either Poitavin (8 grand rue Jean Jaurès) or the several branches of Olmeda, where queues line the pavement on a Saturday morning to pick up this traditional local delicacy ⦿

Gerbeaud

Budapest, Hungary

📍 Vörösmarty tér 7–8, 1051
Budapest, Hungary
🔖 gerbeaud.hu

His sweet offerings attracted the likes of Franz Liszt to linger over coffee and cake.

An institution in the heart of Budapest, Gerbeaud is a veritable palace of confectionery. It was founded in 1858, the same year that its current home was commissioned, originally as a bank. Swiss confectioner Henrik Kugler first set up shop around the corner on Nádor tér, where his sweet offerings attracted the likes of Franz Liszt to linger over coffee and cake. The business moved to the current location, and Kugler went into partnership with fellow compatriot Emil Gerbeaud.

Business boomed and by 1900 a staff of 150 served customers over three floors, who were kept interested by original creations, such as the Gerbeaud szelet, a chocolate-topped slice consisting of pastry layered with own-made apricot jam and crushed walnuts.

These days, the multi-roomed café is patrolled by attentive, brightly waistcoated staff, serving Sachertorte and Eszterházy cake to an eager crowd. Though it's a tourist magnet (note the entire front counter awash with presentation boxes), it's not a tourist trap – there are plenty of locals in the mix, too. Many of the revered Hungarian desserts, such as the Gerbeaud palacsinta (a pancake with a walnut cream filling, thick chocolate sauce and apricot ragout) and the Somlói galuska (a sponge with Tokaji-soaked raisins and chocolate sauce), have a suggested wine accompaniment, invariably a sweet Tokaji Aszú. The kehely (sundaes) are works of art and use homemade ice cream without colourings or additives.

There are also breakfasts and superior daytime snacks – but that's not why you're here.

In summer, the buzzy terrace transforms this otherwise shabbily commercial main square. Through December, when there's a Christmas market on the square, the festive scene is enhanced by a building-sized advent calendar displayed on the Gerbeaud façade ◉

Gragger

Vienna, Austria

📍 Spiegelgaße 23, 1010
Vienna, Austria

⚲ gragger.at

The wood-burning oven here is pretty special. Not only does it produce quality baked goods, but it's also key to Gragger's programme of social engagement.

Helmut Gragger, a former baker's apprentice from Strobl am Wolfgangsee near Salzburg, built his impressive bakery business from scratch. He now has several shops to his name; the most recent opened in March 2018 in the bohemian quarter around Josefstädter Straße, but the flagship store is this one on Spiegelgaße, in the centre of Vienna.

The wood-burning oven here is pretty special. It's an energy-efficient model developed in house: not only does it produce quality baked goods, but it's also key to Gragger's programme of social engagement. His BackMa's charity, based near Linz, trains disadvantaged youngsters to be bakers, and he's also taken his oven to Senegal and Thailand to kick-start collaborative charity projects in those countries.

In Spiegelgaße, more than half a dozen types of bread are baked in the oven, all sourdough and all organic. They include a rye wholemeal (with cumin, fennel, coriander and sea salt) – one of the most popular loaves – and a seed-packed spelt loaf (with 50 per cent wholemeal rye flour, sunflower seeds, pumpkin seeds, flaxseeds and sea salt). This is bread that will last, if properly stored at room temperature, wrapped in lightly moistened natural linen rather than hermetically sealed in plastic or metal boxes.

Equal care is taken over the varieties of Handsemmel (bread rolls), made by hand at a rate of 350 an hour. There are also Beugerls (like bagels) with poppy-seed or nuts, bundt cakes, little individual tarts and Linzer cookies with redcurrant jam. It makes for a tempting display, and the baked goods are indeed the stars of the show. By contrast, décor is minimal – just simple browns and creams, and a scattering of tables here at the Spiegelgaße branch ⊙

Güntherska Hovkonditori & Schweizeri

Uppsala, Sweden

◉ Östra Ågatan 31, 753 22 Uppsala, Sweden

↟ guntherska.se

In semlor season (January to March), Güntherska offers no fewer than nine varieties of the cream bun.

This is one of the most venerable pastry shops in Sweden – in business since 1870 – and is currently owned by the fifth generation of the Landing family. Today, Güntherska consists of a bakery, a pastry shop, a café and a restaurant and is an institution in the university town of Uppsala. It's right by the Fyrisån river, and has pretty views. *Hovkonditori* means 'royal supplier' and the premises live up to that image – it's worth visiting just for the crystal chandeliers and the grand nineteenth-century décor. Service is always charming and friendly, too.

The best sandwiches in town are served here, using own-made sourdough bread of course, and the green pea soup with shrimp is famous. But most of all, it's a wonderful place to explore Sweden's pastry and baking traditions. The range goes from elegant cakes (so lovely they're almost works of art), through pastries and buns, to chocolates and ice cream. The wedding cakes are so beautiful they could tempt you to take the plunge. An everyday order – though heavenly enough – is the shrimp-filled croissant with homemade mayonnaise, followed by a hallondröm (raspberry dream) with chocolate, vanilla mousse and raspberry cream, and a hot chocolate made with melted Valrhona. If indecision strikes in front of the gigantic counter, opt for a selection of miniature confections. In semlor season (January to March), Güntherska offers no fewer than nine varieties of the cream bun. You might have to queue to eat here, but you won't regret it ◉

Hambleton Bakery

Exton, England

⚲ 2 Cottesmore Road,
Exton, Rutland LE15 8AN,
England
⚲ hambletonbakery.co.uk

The Hambleton Local is a revived classic, which uses local beer barm and white and wholemeal flour from nearby Whissendine Mill.

The bakery was originally started by Julian Carter and Tim Hart in 2008 in order to supply Hambleton Hall and Hart's Nottingham; both luxury hotels with classy restaurants that required quality bread. They wanted to produce traditional bread, without additives, using local ingredients where possible. Most of the loaves produced by the bakery today use stone-ground flour, water and salt, which in combination with slow fermentation means longer lasting and distinctive tasting bread. Since then, the business has grown to include a roster of wholesale customers and six local shops (here in Exton, site of the bakery, and others in nearby Oakham, Market Harborough, West Bridgford, Stamford and Oundle). The shops are unflashy but well-stocked and all of them carry the full range of baked goods.

Loaves range from a white crusty round – a real English farmhouse-style bread – to a Russian rye bread with malt and coriander seeds, the Borodinsky. The sourdough is a mix of rye and wheat flour, fermented for forty-eight hours; the Hambleton Local is a revived classic, which uses local beer barm and white and wholemeal flour from nearby Whissendine Mill. There are rolls, and teatime treats too: sourdough pikelets, teacakes and English muffins. Sweet stuff includes the ideal iced bun, brownies, Eccles cakes, filled tarts and Swedish apple cake. Specials appear throughout the year – chocolate ganache and raspberry hearts for Valentine's day, for example, or mince pies (made with their own mincemeat) at Christmas and hot cross buns around Easter. Savouries run from scones (maybe cheese, chive and red onion), to quiches, pies and sausage rolls, and not forgetting the irresistible cheese straw made with Lincolnshire Poacher cheese. There's an attractive energy to the business – a different bread of the month, or new creations keep things fresh, such as the dairy-free courgette and lime cake ◦

Hartog's Volkoren

Amsterdam, Netherlands

⦿ Wibautstraat 77, 1091 GK
Amsterdam, Netherlands
⚓ volkorenbrood.nl

A quintessential
Amsterdam experience.

Hartog's Volkoren has been making bread using the same method for more than a century. Breadmaking trends have, of course, come and gone in this time, but the bakery's focus on the local and wholesome (volkoren is Dutch for 'wholemeal') is much in line with current ideals – which helps explain the queues out the door of this unassuming modern building on Wibautstraat in Amsterdam-Oost. (Hartog's moved here in 2016; the former building at Ruyschstraat 56, a two-minute walk away, now houses the ovens.) Though it's a huge structure, the actual shop part is confined to a small take-away only space in the middle. The rest of the complex houses the on-site mill, where the Dutch wheat is ground daily and then combined – with the undiscarded bran and wheatgerm – with just water, salt and yeast, without any preservatives or improvers, and baked to

make the same bread that Aagje and Gerrit Hartog were first producing back in 1896.

This original bruin brood loaf, with its slightly sweet taste and crispy crust, is still much celebrated, but the range has now extended to include raisin, spelt, seeded, rye and muesli loaves, arranged in an appealingly utilitarian manner on baker's racks behind the counter.

Hartog's isn't just about the bread, though – a variety of crackers and gingerbreads are also available, alongside wholemeal rolls, croissants and biscuits, apple pies and eierkoeken (traditional Dutch 'egg cakes'), as well as the bakery's popular own-made peanut butter and a range of packaged nuts and seeds.

Though there are no interior tables, in line with the unpretentious spirit there is a self-service coffee machine and a wooden

bench out front where you can perch among the town bikes belonging to locals of all stripes. It may not be the most idyllic spot, facing a main traffic artery, but it's a quintessential Amsterdam experience. And if you'd like to immerse yourself further, you can sign up to one of Hartog's popular breadmaking workshops ⦿

Haxby Bakehouse

York, England

📍 8 Ryedale Court, Haxby,
York YO32 3SA, England
🔖 haxbybakehouse.co.uk

Philip Clayton is the baker here, and his bread is proper 100 per cent Yorkshire bread.

Philip Clayton is the baker here, and his bread is proper 100 per cent Yorkshire bread. Much of his flour is milled up the road at Spaunton by the redoubtable Yorkshire Organic Millers and is turned into the kind of loaves that frequently win prizes (World Bread Awards, Great Taste Awards, Yorkshire Life Best Producer Award). Clayton's loaf story is an inspiration for all those who've ever dreamed that their carefully tended sourdough starter could lead to something big. In fact, while Phil tells us his story, he's beginning to feed the last remaining 500g of starter in a two-day augmentation process that will lead to hundreds of loaves of his bestselling pain de levain. This classic, flavourful sourdough bread sells to hordes of Saturday customers, both at his shop and the Bakehouse's stalls at local farmers' markets.

'I start feeding up this starter now, so that by Saturday I'll have about 10kg of levain dough by the end of the long, slow fermentation process. The baking starts in the early hours, and we have a team of three of us working non-stop to produce about 1,000 loaves.'

It's a labour of love that has reaped huge rewards, and is a far cry from the career in retail management he left a decade ago, when, despairing at the lack of good, nutritious breads available for the family's lunchboxes, he decided to learn how to make his own. He studied breadmaking under Andrew Whitley, co-founder of the Real Bread Campaign, and was hooked. When he discovered the empty former health food shop (with a handy bakery at the back) was up for sale, he took a punt that the rest of Haxby (just outside the city of York) would feel like he does about daily bread, and they haven't let him down.

As well as the sourdough, Phil also produces a more leisurely fermented yeasted dough for wholemeal and white crusty loaves. While the bread bakes, these industrious artisans are knocking up light, flaky croissants and brioches, as well as a much-praised focaccia, which they load up with cheese, tomatoes, onions and seasonal vegetables for the lunchtime crowd ●

Hobbs House Bakery

Bristol, England

⊙ 39 High Street, Chipping Sodbury, Bristol BS37 6BA, England

⚲ hobbshousebakery.co.uk

For afternoon tea, you can't go far wrong with a slice of the Bakewell tart.

Like many of today's artisanal bakers, Hobbs House's success comes from pointedly eschewing the Chorleywood Process (the fast baking, high yeast and hard fat method of baking introduced in 1961). To the Herbert family, whose ancestors founded the original bakery that spawned this, the first branch, and its five siblings in Nailsworth, Malmesbury, Tetbury and Bristol (two branches), such 'bread' isn't worthy of the name. Before the Chorleywood method became the norm, a loaf could cost as much as a pint of beer. When that loaf is created from a historic, sixty-three-year-old sourdough starter, carefully augmented and fermented, then shaped and baked to make the moist, chewy crusted loaves that scent this glorious bakery, it's much more valuable than a pint. Investing in their gift pack gives the rookie baker everything needed (including some hallowed celebrity Herbert starter) to become part of the sourdough nation. Bestselling loaves include the floury Sherston white and the crunchy seeded sourdough, but there's a huge variety of spelt, rye, dark and light breads, all fine enough to become the star of any meal. Weekends see a lot of interest in the shiny, rich brioche loaves.

Cake-wise, the fantastic brownies in a variety of flavours attract a great deal of attention, as do the sweet and generously proportioned hikers' fruit bars. For afternoon tea, you can't go far wrong with a slice of the Bakewell tart or a couple of their oft-praised Portuguese custard tarts. In their bid to spread the word about the therapeutic nature of baking, Hobbs House run a wide variety of courses, including their informative day-long Sourdough for Beginners ⊙

Hofbäckerei Edegger-Tax

Graz, Austria

♀ Hofgasse 6, 8010 Graz, Austria

♪ hofbaeckerei.at

Royal approval was gained in 1888 and a double-headed imperial eagle carved over the bakery doorway.

The striking signage on the historic façade of the Edegger-Tax bakery points to an illustrious heritage, but doesn't quite tell the whole story. 'Since 1569' indicates an impressive 450 years of providing bread, yet this bakery was in operation around the corner at Sporgasse 15 for some two centuries beforehand, making it one of the oldest of its kind in Austria. The date shown refers to the year wealthy denizen Peter Veit took over the bakery and, crucially, the mill nearby. The bakery passed into the hands of the Tax family in 1787; royal approval was gained in 1888 and a double-headed imperial eagle carved over the bakery doorway.

Local entrepreneur Franz Edegger married into the family after World War II, and the business gained a name and added a café. To this day, the Hofbäckerei Edegger-Tax remains a family concern, run by Robert Edegger with his mother Walheide, his wife Brigitte and son Matthias all pitching in. Robert has overseen two major renovations, introduced gluten-free alternatives and played up the bakery's heritage with items such as the Sissibusserl, 'Elisabeth's Kisses'. These light, macaron-type delicacies with apricot jam, hazelnut and chocolate stripes, are sold in presentation boxes bearing a likeness of the tragic Bavarian empress. The dainty, almond-flavoured Kaiserzwieback biscuits echo the royal visit of 1883. (The bakery's Habsburg allure has proved so successful that an outpost of Edegger-Tax opened in Tokyo in 2015.) It doesn't hurt the tourist trade that the bakery is right in the heart of Graz, near the medieval Catholic church, but streams of locals also pop in to pick up more everyday items: black and white breads, Salzstangerl long rolls, Topfentascherl curd pastries or maybe a selection of vanilla Kipferl ●

Hofpfisterei

Munich, Germany

⊙ Viktualienmarkt 5, 80331
Munich, Germany

⚲ hofpfisterei.de

Hofpfisterei's breads are three-stage Natursauerteig-Laibe (natural sourdough loaves) made with organic ingredients.

First mentioned in 1331, the Hofpfisterei is Bavaria's oldest bakery. Nicole Stocker took over the business from her father in 2016, ninety-nine years after her grandfather Ludwig first rented the original premises (just as his predecessors had) from the royal administration of the Crown, Nicole's parents expanded the Hofpfisterei into one of Germany's most important organic businesses, committed to social responsibility and sustainability, and one that produces over 20,000 loaves each day.

The Hofpfisterei's breads are three-stage Natursauerteig-Laibe (natural sourdough loaves). They take their baking very seriously here, embracing old craftsmanship laws and a slow, elaborate baking process that takes up to twenty-four hours, and avoids artificial and chemical additives. Over twenty varieties of bread are sold, mostly rye, but other single- and mixed-grain breads, too. Traditional loaves include the Pfister Öko-Bauernbrot dunkel, a rustic dark, coarse rye bread, while more modern options include the Pfister Öko-Dinkel-Hirse, a crusty, nutty spelt-millet-rye bread, and the Pfister Öko-Karotten-Sesambrot, a rye and wheat bread with carrot, sesame and pumpkin seeds.

There are bread rolls aplenty, created from the same variety of grains and sprinkled with a multitude of nuts, seeds and spices, from pine nuts to caraway. The pretzel selection includes the familiar twisted classic baked with cheese, a large, squishy version formed in a thick plait, and even a pretzel croissant. There are excellent sweet baked goods too, from German classics such as Marmorkuchen (marble cake) and Krapfen (doughnuts, here filled with apricot jam), to a good range of pastries dotted with nuts, raisins and poppy seeds.

There are now hundreds of Hofpfisterei outlets – modern looking bakeries with white walls, huge windows and lovely wooden counters – all over Germany, but it remains a Bavarian institution and a Munich staple. The branch at the Viktualienmarkt, is in a prime location: buy a bread roll or a couple of slices of bread from the bakery, find some cheese and a bunch of radishes at a nearby stall, and toast your picnic lunch with a beer at the Viktualienmarkt's leafy beer garden ⊙

Ian's Home Bakery

Belfast, Northern Ireland

9 6 Rosetta Road, Belfast
BT6 0LT, Northern Ireland
+44 28 9064 3192

'We make good old-fashioned breads and cakes which people know and love.'

Soda bread, wheaten loaves and potato farls are the traditional breads of Ireland. They are simple, unleavened breads, made with differing combinations of strong flour, buttermilk and potato but without fat or yeast. All three breads feature on every Irish menu offering a cooked breakfast, and are made daily in home bakeries from coast to coast – these small, hands-on establishments bake the loaves they sell, and offer a range of traditional favourites.

These are the type of breads that are centre stage here at Ian's Home Bakery in south Belfast, and also at Roy's Home Bakery on Kings Square in the east of the city. These are modest, neighbourhood bakeries, run by a father (Roy) and son (Ian) combo, and in business for more than four decades. The no-frills shop windows reflect their genuine and unswerving adherence to what they know best: local favourites for local tastebuds.

The ovens and griddles start operating at 3am, six days a week. The potato and soda bread mixes are left to gather strength before being formed into patties, then cut into farls (quarters). They're placed on a piping hot griddle, then turned until done. Ian's potato farls are dense and intensely flavoured, but not stodgy or gluey, they are just the right thickness, with a subtle but unmistakable potato taste. The floury soda farls are puffy and light, perfect eaten fresh off the griddle, with just a knob of butter. Buy them to take away, or enjoy them in the café with an Ulster Fry (soda bread, potato farl, pancake, bacon, fried egg and tomato).

Ian's basic buns and biscuits have been household favourites for decades too: cubes of simple airy sponge covered in jam and dipped in coconut, and plain biscuits with a blob of snow white

icing and a shiny red cherry on top. There's nothing more elaborate than a chocolate brownie on offer here because, as Janine, who has been working at Ian's Home Bakery for nearly twenty years, explains, their reputation is for the old favourites: 'We make good old-fashioned breads and cakes which people know and love.'

Father and son are clearly doing something right: their breads, muffins and scones are being snapped up by a growing number of outlets across Northern Ireland, including service stations, hotels and restaurants. They even supplied cast and crew during the filming of *Game of Thrones* o

Ille Brød

Oslo, Norway

◉ Lakkegata 53, 0561 Oslo, Norway

⚑ illebrod.no

The smell of the bread, the crunch of the crust and the taste of the moist crumb is out of this world.

New-wave bakers – the ones who focus on freshly milled local and ancient grains, and who concentrate on taste over yield – have become stars in recent years. The breed is exemplified by Martin Fjeld, a former student turned hobby baker turned bread prodigy, who has taken the Oslo bread scene by storm with his A-grade artisan breadmaking. He uses flour milled less than forty minutes away from his small bakery, and is on a mission to bring back the understanding of bread as a meal in itself. Bread has everything you need, he claims, as long as the dough has time to develop its flavours and release the nutrients in the grains. He also has plans to acquire a stone mill for the bakery, which will be placed where one of two tables sit today.

The stripped-down premises give little hint of the rich pickings contained within, but loyal customers ensure that Ille Brød regularly sells out of loaves before lunchtime, so get there early if you want a choice. There's only a small range to start with – a few types of bread (sourdough, with various percentages of wholegrain, plus spelt and malt), a selection of rolls and the odd pastry, such as a cinnamon knot. But the smell of the bread, the crunch of the crust and the taste of the moist crumb is out of this world. Once a month, Ille Brød serves pizza with creative toppings: the likes of cheese, ham, pickled root celery and juniper berries sit on top of a glorious dough that bakes to give a crust with a bite. It's addictive stuff.

The name Ille Brød comes from a well-known expression from Martin's home town, Fredrikstad; the literal translation is 'bad bread', but it really means 'fantastic bread' – and it's no exaggeration ◦

Isabella Glutenfreie Patisserie

Düsseldorf, Germany

♀ Arnulfstraße 4, 40545 Düsseldorf, Germany
➤ isabella-patisserie.de

Isabella Krätz refused to abandon her love of patisserie and freshly baked bread after she was diagnosed with coeliac disease.

Isabella Krätz refused to abandon her love of patisserie and freshly baked bread after she was diagnosed with coeliac disease. She travelled across Europe and to the US, visiting coeliac-friendly patisseries and tasting their gluten-free offerings, then studied under renowned pastry chefs and completed her master craftsman's exams before opening Düsseldorf's first gluten-free patisserie in 2015. She's worked tirelessly to produce breads and petits fours that are every bit as good as their traditional counterparts and, with her husband and two sons, Isabella now runs four sites in Germany, offering not just high-end gluten-free products but also lactose-free and vegan goods, too.

Isabella's gluten-free breads are made with organic flour and baked fresh every day; the generous selection includes traditional mixed loaves such as linseed bread (Leinsamenbrot), and low-carb options like protein bread (Proteinbrot). There's also a good variety of bread rolls. The display of beautiful cakes and tartlets is based on a rotation of fifty different offerings, from passionfruit mousse tart to white chocolate cheesecake, macarons to eclairs and vegan fruit tartlets.

The savoury selection is impressive: the quiches are excellent (the salmon in particular), and there are classy sandwiches, and focaccia rich with tomato, buffalo mozzarella and fresh basil. Eat-in breakfast options include bread rolls with cheeses and cold cuts, and a homemade vegan granola. If you stop for coffee, there's a choice of milks, with the treat of a Sicilian biscotti alongside.

The patisserie is a passion project for Isabella, and her attention to detail is striking, from the glass counter filled with lovingly decorated sweets to the interior décor of the café, which feels cosy and welcoming despite its contemporary look. The staff are knowledgeable and friendly too, and happy to discuss the baked goods ●

Joseph Brot vom Pheinsten

Vienna, Austria

○ Naglergasse 9, 1010 Vienna, Austria
▴ joseph.co.at

Organic chestnut Guglhupf cake, a classic redolent of Central Europe.

Ten years ago, Josef Weghaupt – ex-butcher, qualified food technologist and marketing man for a major bread manufacturer – opened a modest artisanal bakery in a bucolic location in his native region of Waldviertel (north-west of Vienna, towards the Czech border). In partnership with traditional baker Friedrich Potočnik, he began to produce organic sourdough bread, refining a process that involves fermentation over forty-eight hours, then baking and re-baking.

Customers liked the results, and the business flourished. Counting in Weghaupt's favour was not only the quality of the product, but also his marketing savvy. The firm became Joseph Brot vom Pheinsten (Brot vom Feinsten means 'bread at its finest', with the 'ph' a cute nod to a more old-fashioned form of German), and people, including the press, picked up on the concept before they'd even tasted the sourdough's caramelised crust.

The partners took the brand to Vienna in 2011, moving into these premises on Naglergasse surrounded by fashion houses, jewellers and the venerable Esterhazykeller restaurant. Their Brotboutique was soon selling rustic loaves in bags that read *Ideal für Stadt-Menschen* ('Ideal for City People'). Two years later, the Joseph Bakery, Patisserie, Bistro opened on Landstraße, not only selling bread and patisserie, but also providing a deli outlet for organic producers from the Waldviertel. Today, there's also a bagel and cake outlet on tourist-choked Albertinaplatz, a bakery-patisserie in the Döbling area of the city, and a thriving wholesale business supplying high-end restaurants. Back in the Waldviertel, there's now a large bakery in Burgschleinitz, where visitors can watch thirty-five craftsmen at work.

At the Naglergasse store, the range of loaves has grown to include the likes of pumpkin seed, honey and lavender rye, olive and tomato ciabatta with rosemary, spelt with grape juice and rye with puréed organic Topaz summer apples, a speciality of the Czech/Austrian border region. You can also pick up organic chestnut Guglhupf cake, a classic redolent of Central Europe, and organic butter croissants with Zotter chocolate from Styria ○

Korica

Zagreb, Croatia

⚲ Preradovićeva 39, 10000
Zagreb, Croatia
⚑ korica.hr

The cruffin – a recently created
croissant/muffin hybrid that Croatia
is claiming as its own – is sold here.

After seeing artisan bakeries open all over Europe, entrepreneur Ivana Urem Marohnić decided that Zagreb needed one too. While the baking methods are time-honoured, Ivana knew that the business needed a cutting edge look to compete with Zagreb's chicest cafés for attention. She got local designers Diorama to create a chic interior of shining stainless steel, with plenty of natural light and copper pendant lamps dangling from the ceiling. Ivana also chose the location

with care – Preradovićeva, a pedestrianised stretch off the main square by the flower market, is popular with Zagreb's creatives, who gather there to talk shop while sipping sugary coffee. Above all though, the bread is the star of the show: flour, water, yeast, salt and a fermentation time of up to forty-eight hours lie behind everything from rye sourdough to nut and raisin bread. *Zagrepčani* have been quick to show their appreciation, posting Instagram snaps of their bounty. As well as the

loaves, there are mini quiches, apple pies, cookies, banana bread, lemon and poppy seed cake and marble bread. Croissants (plain and almond) fly off the shelves in the pre-work rush, while brioches, with or without raisins, do a roaring trade mid-morning and mid-afternoon. The cruffin – a recently created croissant/muffin hybrid that Croatia is claiming as its own – is sold here, too. Children, however, still go for old-fashioned treats such as pains au chocolat and chocolate cookies ○

Kruščić

Split, Croatia

⌖ Obrov ulica 6, 21000 Split, Croatia
☎ +385 99 261 2345

Occasionally a sack of flour is delivered from a small, family-run watermill just outside Split.

There's a story behind every bakery and Kruščić, by the gutted Roman palace comprising the historic centre of Split, has a particularly twisting tale.

In the 1980s, while travelling in India, Anand Štambuk came across a German bakery in Pune. For him it was a revelation, as he was used to state-controlled bread in his native Yugoslavia. The idea to set up something similar back home led him to Hubert, a traditional German baker in Baden-Württemberg, south-west Germany. They decided to go into business, but war intervened, and it was almost twenty years later that Štambuk (with Hubert, who had married a Croatian) finally set up Kruščić ('little bread').

A busy little store with charming, chatty staff, Kruščić is near the fish market, a few paces from the Adriatic. It's easy to spot, with a handwritten shop sign and a statuette of an exotic bird outside. Inside are shelves groaning with artisanal bread and a display case of cakes and pastries; there's also a little bakery at the back. Occasionally a sack of flour is delivered from a small, family-run watermill just outside Split, alongside the Žrnovica river (and known in Split as a location in *Game of Thrones*).

Loaves of dark, crusty bracera fly off the shelves – this half-rye, half-wheat combination is the most popular choice among regulars. Unleavened rye is another favourite, while rosemary bread with almonds (ružica sa bademima) or with cheese (ružica sa sirom) have their fans too. Spread out on the serving counter is a large tray of kruščička pogača, sliced into squares for take-away consumption – this savoury snack is the bakery's own take on the better known viška pogača, an anchovy and tomato focaccia pie from the island of Vis. Alongside are crusty sandwiches, ideal for a picnic on Bačvice beach or for taking aboard one of the many boats headed for the nearby islands ⦿

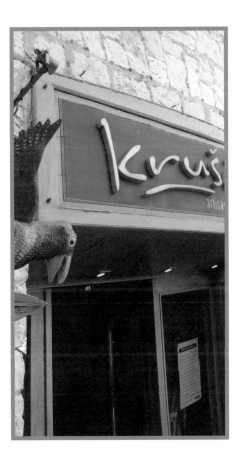

Lanskroon

Amsterdam, Netherlands

♀ Singel 385, 1012 WL
Amsterdam, Netherlands
↟ lanskroon.nl

Those with a serious stroopwafel addiction can order a box of six to take away.

Locals will cross town for Lanskroon's stroopwafels, the thin, crispy waffle discs with gooey syrup fillings that are perhaps Holland's best sweet creation. This little corner bakery-café on the Singel canalside, near the Spui square, makes these delicious treats on the premises: the classic caramel and honey kinds, as well as the less familiar fig paste and coffee- or cinnamon-caramel varieties.

Owner Claudia Dunselman, a fourth-generation pastry chef, took over the running of Lanskroon from her parents in 1999, giving it a modern twist with the introduction of new items, such as the home-made fruit and nut-filled ice creams in spring and summer (the result of time spent travelling in Italy). Yet the place remains resolutely Dutch; it's straightforward, with a friendly, down-to-earth atmosphere, canary-yellow walls and simple wooden furniture.

Local specialities include gevulde koeken (almond cookies), gemberkoek (ginger and almond cake), appelcitroenvlaai (apple and lemon tart), oliebollen (Dutch doughnuts, traditionally eaten at New Year) and spiced speculaas (Christmas cookies). Savoury options, such as kaasbroodje (cheese-filled pastry), sausage rolls and vegetable turnovers, are displayed in a modern glass counter at the back.

But back to the stroopwafels, the incredibly moreish stars of the show. To enjoy them at the perfect temperature and consistency, the trick is to put the round discs on top of your mug of coffee, hot chocolate or tea – all excellent here – for a minute or two so that they gently soften with the steam, giving the inside layer exactly the right gooeyness. This is harder to do with Lanskroon's dessert-plate sized konigs stroopwafels (kingsize

syrup waffles), the most indulgent option. Those with a serious stroopwafel addiction can order a box of six to take away ●

Leakers

Bridport, England

📍 29 East Street, Bridport,
Dorset DT6 3JX, England

📍 leakersbakery.co.uk

Leakers is proudly Dorset – check out
the Jurassic Foot crunchy date loaf,
shaped like a dinosaur's footprint.

G.S. Leaker opened his bakery on East Street in 1914, having moved to Dorset from Devon, and sweated over the old coal-fired ovens to produce fabulous breakfast loaves, while proving his cake artistry with a sideline in elaborate wedding cakes. Today, Leakers is riding the crest of the artisanal baking wave and has been a consistent winner in the Great Taste Awards for many years. Although the brick-based ovens no longer run on coal, and the bakery's current owners are no longer from the Leaker family, the shop at the front retains many of its fittings from a revamp in the 1950s, giving it a comfortingly old-school air. Its products are bang on trend for today's tastes, though – Leakers even produces a vegetarian lardy cake (alongside the glistening, sugary, larded version, of course). More obviously wholesome is the multi award-winning five-seeded malted sourdough,

whose crunchy crust comes from a wealth of seedy goodness: linseed, sunflower, quinoa, sesame and millet.

Leakers is proudly Dorset – check out the Jurassic Foot crunchy date loaf, shaped like a dinosaur's footprint, and a tribute to the fossil-rich Jurassic coastline two miles away at West Bay. The cheese and cider loaf is a celebration of local rolling pastures and picturesque orchards, as is the traditional apple cake, made to a century-old recipe handed down through the Leaker family. The flour is from Stoates Cann Mill, while the delicious additions to the savoury breads and pastries come from Olives et Al, down the road in Sturminster, as well as Chesil Smokery and Manor Organic Farm. And, true to local tradition, Leakers will also sell you a tin of Dorset Knobs (sure to raise a giggle when they're brought out for the cheese board) ○

Levain

Helsinki, Finland

◊ Kankurinkatu 6, 00150
Helsinki, Finland

↟ levain.fi

Purity of ingredients – local
where possible – is important.

Bakers Kaisa Johansson and Susanna Vuori draw their sourdough inspiration from bakeries in Nordic neighbours Copenhagen and Stockholm, as well as from further afield in central Europe and west coast USA. As part of a trend that has seen bakers and pastry chefs sharing expertise and creativity across the world, their experience includes spells at Helsinki's (now defunct) Michelin star pioneer Chez Dominique. Their CVs also list L'Atelier de Joël Robuchon (London), sourdough tutorship from Sébastien Boudet (Stockholm), and leading culinary institute Ferrandi (Paris), while their kitchen team has a similarly impressive and varied background.

So much for the credentials, but what about the product? Purity of ingredients – local where possible – is important. Sourdough cultures that eschew industrial baking yeasts are the base for a range of wonderful crusty breads baked in a stone oven. The list includes a Danish rye made with rye flour, malted rye, toasted sunflower and pumpkin seeds and ancient grains (here spelt and einkorn as well as heirloom wheat). Baguettes, brioche rolls and seeded crackers also feature.

Sweet treats include mouthwateringly good croissants and pasteis de nata, as well as teacakes; savouries feature rolls generously packed with anything from avocado and grilled aubergine to pastrami and cold smoked salmon, and there are pies with fillings that change with the season.

Levain is a 'bakery-eatery', and the eatery side of the business offers breakfast, lunch and evening meals. The all-day Saturday breakfast features a winning mix of local yoghurt and granola, toast (using the sourdough of the day) with various toppings, plus waffles and smoothies. It's is the kind of inventive, original and easy-going place that Helsinki had lacked and quickly grew to love, and in spring 2018 a second branch opened in the Töölö district, north-west of the city centre ○

Leve

Malmö, Sweden

Östra Rönneholmsvägen 6, 21147 Malmö, Sweden
bagerileve.se

The signature tartelettes are beautiful – seasonal specials include an amazing sea buckthorn meringue.

Baker Martin Westin and pastry chef Didrik Persson have been the talk of Malmö since they opened Leve, close to Triangeln Square in the centre of town. Not only because they have adjusted the baker's clock to provide freshly baked bread in the afternoon when people are on their way home from work as well as in the morning, but also because of their fabulous Friday doughnuts. Creatively flavoured and 100 per cent vegan, they're so popular that people line up outside the bakery to get their hands on one straight from the fryer. Strawberry-elderflower, coffee-chocolate, crème brûlée and mojito are just a selection of recent flavours.

Worthier, but just as wonderful, is the crusty sourdough bread. Baked in many forms, the loaves are made with local organic flour, left to rise for many hours and baked in a stone oven. The baguettes are also good and so is the Skanian kavring rye bread, flavoured with malt syrup and cumin. The signature tartelettes are beautiful – seasonal specials include an amazing sea buckthorn meringue. Butterscotch buns, pains au chocolat and pasteis de nata are other must-trys. Savoury pastries come with innovative toppings, such as crème fraîche, kale, lemon, garlic and cheese. Leve is mainly a shop, but there are a few tables for those who want to enjoy a well-executed coffee from the local roasters, Solde ⊙

The Loaf

San Sebastián, Spain

Avenida de la Zurriola 18, 20002 San Sebastián, Spain
+34 943 26 50 30

The Basic, a white flour loaf, is the one found in bread baskets across the city's Michelin-starred restaurants.

The Loaf began as (and remains) an anomaly among the bakeries in the north of Spain. Three friends (including current owner Xabier de la Maza) dreamed of bringing artisan baking back to San Sebastián after the industrialisation of the bread industry in the twentieth century. And they did so in 2012, in the most modern way possible – a pop-up. A pair of shipping containers, outfitted with ovens and staffed by bakers in white aprons, bedded down on the banks of the Urumea river for a summer. Locals were initially bewildered by the hand-made loaves that used a sourdough starter, but the experiment was a success, and in 2014 a bricks-and-mortar location opened at Zurriola beach.

From the beginning, bread was the star. Made using only organic, stone-milled flours, and all-natural sourdough starter, with a long fermentation process, the resulting loaves have a distinctive flavour and texture, and are a world apart from the Styrofoam-like baguettes found across town. The bestseller is the Extreme, a mixture of white, wholewheat and rye flours (all organic, all Spanish), stone-ground, and fermented for twenty-four hours. If the chewy sourness doesn't suit, there are twenty more types on offer, including campagne, corn, classic baguette, turmeric, spelt, white loaf sandwich bread, and more. The Basic, a white flour loaf, is the one found in bread baskets across the city's Michelin-starred restaurants, from Mugaritz to Martín Berasategui.

There are six shops in San Sebastián now, but the original on the Zurriola is the largest. Breads line the wall, while the counter is covered in baked goods, most with an American bent. Nestled among the carrot cake, chocolate chip cookies and brownies, however, is the most delicious croissant – made with French butter, it's one of the city's best. There's room to sit and eat your croissant or toasted bread, perhaps accompanied by award-winning Cal Saboi olive oil or local jams, plus a freshly squeezed orange juice or an excellent coffee from local roasters Sakona ◦

Lukullus

Warsaw, Poland

📍 Mokotowska 52A, 00-543
Warsaw, Poland
🔖 cukiernialukullus.pl

France remains a major inspiration, and it's where they return at least once a year to keep up with trends.

It may look like a sleek purveyor of the most contemporary cakes and pastries, but Lukullus actually has its roots in 1946, when pastry chef and former chocolatier at famed brand Wedel, Jan Dynowski, founded the firm in war-torn Warsaw. Fast forward two generations, and Dynowski's grandson Albert Judycki is continuing the dynastic tradition. He studied pastry-making at Le Cordon Bleu in Paris, where his fellow Pole (and later business partner) Jacek Malarski graduated from the equally prestigious Ferrandi school.

France remains a major inspiration, and it's where they return at least once a year to keep up with trends. The limoncello tart, for example, takes elements of recipes by Pierre Hermé, Jacques Genin and Cédric Grolet to create a light meringue with a velvety lemon curd. But the pair's transformation of the Lukullus brand hasn't left the past behind – for example, the Baba 96 cake, of egg yolk, vanilla and lemon, is inspired by a recipe found in the nineteenth-century cookbook by Lucyna Ćwierczakiewiczowa, the Mrs Beeton of Poland.

The twenty-first-century incarnation of Lukullus has seven branches in the Polish capital, with everything made at the bakery in Stare Bielany on Warsaw's northern fringes. A mix of cafés and shops includes a handy outlet in the Golden Terrace mall alongside Warszawa Centralna station, and this stylish shop surrounded by jewellery stores on Mokotowska. The most recent offshoot of Lukullus is a chic ice cream parlour in the riverside neighbourhood of Powiśle, which opened in summer 2018.

Whichever Lukullus you visit – all are easily identified by the vibrant yellow branding – the selection laid out on pre-war silver platters will feature viennoiserie, tarts, choux buns, doughnuts and biscuits. A gluten-free cheesecake, takatamatcha, combines citrus jelly (a blend of yuzu, lemon and grapefruit) and matcha green tea, while the Biarritz-Warsaw is based on a recipe from Pariès, the venerable pastry-makers from the French Basque region ◦

Maison Adam

St-Jean-de-Luz, France

📍 6 rue de la République,
64500 St-Jean-de-Luz,
France

⚓ maisonadam.fr

The bakery is still in the family (the twelfth generation) and framed black and white photos and ancient portraits of the Maison Adam clan line the walls.

The macaron comes in many shapes, colours and sizes, from dainty pink rose-scented mouthfuls to bright green pistachio with chocolate sandwiched in between. But at Maison Adam, it has been fetishised in its most basic form: nothing more than ground almond, egg whites and sugar. No colours, no sandwiched cream, no gilding the lily.

Maison Adam's main outlet looks out on St-Jean-de-Luz's liveliest square. Stylish peppers on strings line the exterior in a nod to the region's tradition of hanging them out to dry on farmhouse façades. The space is divided in two, both sides painted a chic black, one selling baked goods and artisanal preserves, the other offering decorative box after decorative box of the mighty macaron (every year or so, the firm commissions another collectable macaron box from a local Basque artist). In the window is a gigantic croquembouche-style display. And these macarons really are unlike any others. They're a uniform shade of vanilla, save the top, which has been evenly browned to a lovely coffee tone, and the crispy edges droop into a chewy, concave centre. The family recipe dates back to 1660, when Louis XIV was apparently a fan, and since then the recipe and process remain as well guarded as the crown jewels. The bakery is still in the family (the twelfth generation) and framed black and white photos and ancient portraits of the Maison Adam clan line the walls.

Apart from macarons, the shop sells a selection of local produce, from paté to *guindilla* peppers. Freshly baked goods include bread, moelleux (a soft chocolate cake), croissants, pain au chocolat and more. A corner is also devoted to a display of perfect squares of chocolate in over thirty-five flavours, ranging from green tea to piment d'Espelette, the piquant pepper grown locally ◦

Maison Aleph

Paris, France

◊ 20 rue de la Verrerie,
Marais, Paris, France
↟ maisonaleph.com

The whole enterprise is
a beautiful fusion of modern
Paris and traditional Syria.

Syrian expatriate Myriam Sabet was devastated by the images of war in her homeland and decided to counter them with something more positive. So she set up a patisserie in Paris, the city she's called home for the last twenty years. To make it happen, she ditched a long-term career in finance, signed on for an NVQ in baking and then flew to Montreal to study under a Syrian master baker. The result is Maison Aleph, opened in July 2017, a petite boutique in the fashionable

Marais. Sabet's artfully crafted small pastries are clever updates on Middle Eastern classics. There are three basic choices: '1001 feuilles' are small squares of stacked filo pastry layered with nuts and fruit, similar to a baklava; 'nids de voyage' are tiny nests of kadayif (angel hair pastry) filled with tangy fruit jellies, nutty pastes or dark chocolate, and, best of all, 'nids pâtissiers' are crunchy whirls of kadayif filled with different pastes and topped with smooth flavoured creams. The flavours are those of Sabet's childhood and include mango, jasmine, cardamom, cinnamon, orange blossom and tamarind. The bestseller is a gorgeously refreshing nids pâtissiers with yoghurt and rosewater.

Maison Aleph also offers its own take on cereal bars, with almonds, sunflower seeds and dried fruits set in kadayif on a milk or dark chocolate base,

as well as bars of high-grade dark chocolate with a twist – pepped up by a studding of tart sumac, for instance. There are even a couple of house-special cold drinks, one made with freshly squeezed Amalfi lemons and another subtly flavoured with rose water.

Like petits fours, Sabet's pasties are small and you need to buy two or three. That, she says, is the whole point: 'It's like mezze, you try lots of different things and experience lots of different flavours.' Locals buy them by the box, sealed in elegant Wedgewood-blue packaging that uses patterns from the courtyard of Aleppo's Grand Mosque. The name of the shop is derived from the same city: Alep is French for Aleppo, Sabet's hometown, and Aleph is also the first letter of the Arabic alphabet. The whole enterprise is, as Sabet intended, a beautiful fusion of modern Paris and traditional Syria ◦

Maison Dandoy

Brussels, Belgium

📍 31 rue au Beurre, 1000 Brussels, Belgium

➤ maisondandoy.com

Part of the pleasure is the sense of history behind the products. The first Maison Dandoy was opened in Brussels in 1829.

Speculoos – delightful little biscuits made with butter and brown sugar and fashioned by old wooden moulds – are the speciality at Maison Dandoy. This crunchy biscuit is a favourite in northern European countries and Maison Dandoy has raised them to an art form: they come in vanilla or cinnamon flavours, with almonds or coated in dark or milk chocolate. This being Brussels, you can even buy them in the shape of the Manneken Pis. Also on offer are chewy biscuits such as Florentines and more yielding ones like macarons. Les biscuits sables are round shortbread cookies which come in all kinds of flavours – pistachio, chocolate and hazelnut, lemon, and vanilla topped with candied angelica. There are little cakes too – financiers and frangipane. Brioche loaves come laden with sugar or dotted with raisins. Dandoy is also known for its pain à la grecque, a heavily sugared biscuit-bread. Yet more sugary stuff can be had in the form of beautifully fashioned marzipan sweets and fruit jellies.

All the exquisite baked goods are still traditionally made in Brussels, and part of the pleasure is the sense of history behind the products. The first Maison Dandoy was opened in Brussels by baker Jean-Baptiste Dandoy in 1829. Today, his descendants have eight shops in Belgium; the oldest remaining store is pleasingly located on the rue au Beurre and looks a treat, especially at Christmas. Head to the Maison Dandoy tearoom on rue Charles Buls to indulge in a waffle ⊙

Maison Villaret

Nîmes, France

9 13 rue de la Madeleine,
30000 Nîmes, France
↟ maison-villaret.com

A café, waffle house, baker of
enormous traditional loaves, maker
of classic patisserie, viennoiserie,
macarons and party pieces,
confectioner, chocolatier, confisseur
and nougatier.

Maison Villaret is highly reputed and distinctly old-school, but that hasn't given it any airs and graces. It just keeps on doing what it's been doing for the last 250 years, working hard for its living from premises on a crossroads deep in the historic centre of Nîmes. It's the complete all-rounder, functioning as a café, waffle house, baker of enormous traditional loaves, maker of classic patisserie, viennoiserie, macarons and party pieces, confectioner, chocolatier, confisseur and nougatier. Its style speaks of fun and full-on flavour rather than too much finesse, nicely evidenced in the marzipan menagerie that inhabits the window display, featuring bright ladybirds and cheeky crabs.

Villaret came into being in 1775 when Claude Villaret, an ambitious baker from nearby Lédignan, took over an existing bakery and gave it his name. As well as bread, he made and sold cakes perfumed with lemon and orange flower, and these proved so popular that Claude's son Jules incorporated the same flavours when devising the recipe for croquants – the almond biscuits for which the bakery became famous.

By the 1790s, croquants were more than simply biscuits. A new decimal system was being introduced amid a currency crisis in the wake of the French Revolution, but the new 'centime' did not allow for any change from the six liard price of a pain au lait. So Villaret staff made up the difference in croquants.

Villaret still makes croquants today, to the original recipe. It's tempting, at first sight of these plain, rectangular rusks, to assume that their suitability for use as a currency derives from their durability in the pocket rather than from any more appetising attributes. This impression persists when, instead of the crunchy texture that the name promises, they deliver more of a chew. But it's a chew that releases intensely aromatic Provençal flavours first captured 200 years ago, giving a glimpse of a time before the advent of refrigeration allowed for fancier pastries. When asked whether croquants remained popular because of their taste or tradition, a member of staff answered: 'les deux'. They are still eaten at feasts and festivals, and used as a currency of courtesy as thanks for a favour or a service.

Most of the tables that line the windows inside are just for two, reflecting Villaret's metier as a quick refuelling point, but they also make a fine spot to linger over a café au lait and observe daily life. For social occasions, customers settle in at the larger tables at the salon de thé next door, which features the same menu (including ten teas), but in fancier (but still not all that fancy) surrounds ◦

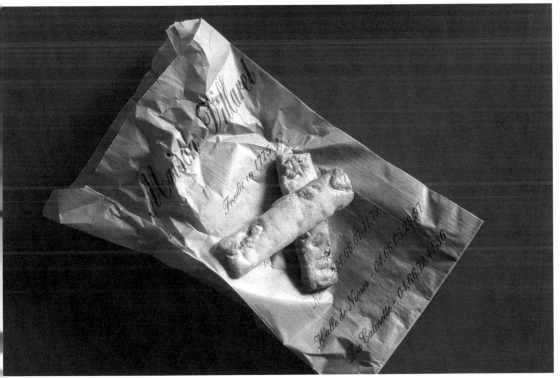

Maison Violette

Avignon, France

📍 30 Place des Corps Saints, 84000 Avignon, France
📞 +33 9 86 47 45 50

Whimsical window displays – a string of breadstick hearts, for example, or a collaged pastry giraffe – which chime with Avignon's artistic heart.

Sweet Violette rises with the lark to catch the morning commuters and continues from breakfast via lunch through to *goûter* (children's tea). This contemporary café/bakery calls itself a 'boulangerie naturelle'. Its founder, Sébastien Beaupère, an Avignon local, trained in Paris but eventually returned home to take over a bakery whose wood-burning oven dates from Roman times. After contemplating the nuances of crust formation, the characteristics of ancient cereals and the ideal bread to partner every dish, he opened Maison Violette first in Avignon's gourmet food hall/market, Les Halles, and then, in 2016, here on place des Corps Saints. This address translates as the Square of the Holy Bodies, which seems appropriate, as Violette's well-to-do, health-conscious clientele appreciate the nutritional benefits of the natural grains and traditional baking methods that Beaupère brings to his range of bread, viennoiserie and patisserie.

Violette works with a range of non-wheat flours, too, and it has become a site of pilgrimage for those who love their baked goods but can't stomach gluten. Treats including croissants, brioches, sablé biscuits, Bordeaux-style canelés and even seasonal delicacies such as Twelfth Night's gâteau de rois feature alternative grains without any compromise in quality. Brioches made with chestnut flour, for instance, somehow manage to be dense and light all at once, not to mention unusually tasty. The dozen or so loaves on sale run the gamut from massive Poilâne-style sourdough wheels to moist, diabetic-friendly seaweed bread to softer, lighter pains de lait, and feature all the fashionable seeds you've ever heard of. As do all the goods here – there's even a chia seed, orange flower and apricot lolly ('the Antioxidant') among the delicious homemade ices.

The bright colour and sense of delight evident in such confections sets the tone for the whimsical window displays – a string of breadstick hearts, for example, or a collaged pastry giraffe – which chime with Avignon's artistic heart (its theatre festival is legendary). Otherwise, the style is simple, with street seating dotted around a dove-grey retro façade and smiley assistants in stripy tops serving an animated crowd and their offspring ●

Maison Weibel

Aix-en-Provence, France

📍 2 rue Chabrier, 13100
Aix-en-Provence, France
⚓ maisonweibel.com

The Aixois, native to the town, is a must-try: it's a diamond-shaped confection with a calisson-based centre and a lavender glaze.

Weibel has been recognised as a patisserie *par excellence* since it was founded by patriarch Georges in 1954. Since then, three generations of master patissiers have curated the company's range of French and Provençal classics, as well as putting their own stamp on it. In 2016, though, Paul Weibel instituted a revamp that transformed it into a brand worthy of national attention. He brought in a new logo and ravishing violet and gold packaging, refined and updated the presentation and redesigned the shop and salon de thé inside and out.

Maison Weibel occupies a key corner of place Richelme, the beating heart of Aix's old town. There's a food and flower market here daily, and the town hall and post office are just a couple of blocks away, so *le tout* Aix has cause to pass by, or, more accurately, stop in. The claw-footed bistro tables wrapped around the outside are always busy, as is the more intimate salon de thé indoors. It's all rather classy, in dove grey, with an elegant black and white tiled floor and waistcoated servers.

The displays proffer a wide range of sweet treats: macarons, petits fours, chocolates, conserves, cakes of all shapes and sizes and a couple of dozen patisseries. The classics are all present and very much correct, but maybe with a little extra decorative gloss, or with contemporary variations: an army of choux pastry réligieuses, perhaps, standing in ranks of hazelnut, raspberry, fruit caramel and chocolate. The Aixois, native to the town, is a must-try: it's a diamond-shaped confection with a calisson-based centre and a lavender glaze. Also consider sampling one of the well-reputed fraisiers or framboisiers, and the house special castel praliné (almond and praline cake). If you're lucky, the refreshing cactus and lemon mousse ball might make a guest appearance.

Like the cakes, Weibel's café fare is a little more aspirational than the average bakery's. Breakfasts might include a gourmet version of the 'full English'; lunches, served in prettily packaged bowls, are simple but cheffy (such as polenta and parsley-stuffed sardines), and afternoon tea is properly presented in three tiers. The ice creams too are creative (and delicious). Flavours include peach and lavender, a sour cherry and Pierre Hermé's invention ispahan (rose, raspberry and lychee).

Don't leave Weibel without some calissons. Calissons d'Aix, to be precise: the almond and fruit paste sweetmeats that originated here in Aix and are now known worldwide. Not only is Weibel one of only thirteen producers to meet the criteria of the appellation, but Paul Weibel is president of the guild of producers, who fight for the trademark worldwide. In 2017, the guild had to act quickly to suppress a threat from China when a company there started to manufacture what they called 'kalisongs'. This protectionism isn't only for economic reasons, but to ensure quality. The *Aixois* calissons use only superior local almonds, and at least 32 per cent of them (Weibel takes that up to 46 per cent) ◦

Mali Princ

Belgrade, Serbia

◆ Palmotićeva 27, 11000
Belgrade, Serbia
⚓ mali-princ.rs

The late opening hours, common to bakeries in the Balkans, lend themselves to romantic rendezvous.

Mali Princ translates as the Little Prince, but this is no themed bakery: the staid interior is decorated in a low key fashion, with no sign of Saint-Exupéry's shock-haired extraterrestrial. What draws customers to this corner café near Belgrade's botanical garden is the ever-changing selection of delicious patisserie, arranged in rows in a display cabinet. The names of the cakes, given in Serbian in Roman script, will mean little to the foreign visitor, but it's easy to point at the object of your desire. Perhaps srce borovnica (heart of blueberries); u iscekivanju sunca (in expectation of the sun), with kiwi fruit, strawberries and wafer-thin layers of cream puff, or ludilo, a champagne, raspberry and orange liqueur concoction.

A lemon cake in some form or other will invariably be in the mix, as will išler (Ischler to Austrians), a layered chocolate cookie cake originally made for Habsburg Emperor Franz Josef upon his visit to Bad Ischl in Austria in 1849 and since found all over his sweet-toothed realm.

Other ornate concoctions are more recent, devised for Mali Princ's thirtieth anniversary celebrations in 2017. Freshly made fruit tarts, set apart from the main display, appear at lunchtimes, and the range of pralines is almost as impressive as the cakes.

The original site of Mali Princ was closer to the city centre, but this more secluded location has the advantage of two quiet, leafy terraces; the late opening hours (until midnight), common to bakeries in the Balkans, lend themselves to romantic rendezvous ◦

Manteigaria

Lisbon, Portugal

📍 Rua do Loreto 2, 1200–108 Lisbon, Portugal
📞 +351 21 347 1492

From the time they leave the oven to the time they're on your lips can be as little as five minutes, just long enough to not burn your mouth.

If you don't know anything about football, the next best way to start up a conversation with a *Lisboeta* is to ask where you can find good pasteis de nata. Opinions vary about which pastelaria is number one, but Manteigaria is on everyone's shortlist. It's a dedicated bakery on a busy road in Bairro Alto, one of Lisbon's smart inner suburbs, and is an easy journey on tram number 28.

The baking aroma wafts down the street and leads you by the nose into a long, narrow room. There's a high counter that does a busy take-away trade with locals, but if you're not a regular, linger awhile inside and watch the baking in progress.

There's not much to Manteigaria's formula: order a cappuccino or espresso and a pastel de nata or two. They arrive immediately. Pay, move down the counter, and watch the bakers at work through the plate glass window. Trays of fresh pasteis are taken from the oven, carefully checked, and then when the tops are caramelised to just the right degree, a bell is rung and they're taken to the front counter. From the time they leave the oven to the time they're on your lips can be as little as five minutes, just long enough to not burn your mouth. The cup is made of flaky pastry with a slight crispness to it; the egg custard just set and evenly textured. Besides the firm egginess of the filling there's a hint of cinnamon – this and the caramelised edges around the top give a very slight bitterness and set these tarts apart. Shakers marked *canela* are provided if you want dust your cake with even more cinnamon.

There is a smaller and less busy branch in the popular Time Out Market in the centre of town; the cakes there are just as good, but the market unit lacks the atmosphere of the original ◦

Marchesi 1824

Milan, Italy

⚲ Via Santa Maria alla
Porta 11a, Milan 20123,
Italy
➤ pasticceriamarchesi.com

Best of all are the paper-wrapped
sourdough panettoni, the airy
Christmas cakes with dry raisins
and candied peel, said to be invented
in fifteenth-century Milan.

Pasticceria Marchesi is located in one of Milan's most beautiful buildings: an eighteenth-century palazzo, whose exterior is carved with elegant sgraffito (designs incised on plaster), in the form of inverted fleurs-de-lis. So it seemed fitting that one of Milan's most iconic fashion brands, Prada, bought 80 per cent of the shares in the venerable bakery and cake shop in 2014, 190 years after its opening in 1824.

Under Prada's guidance, Marchesi has recently opened two stylish new shops – one on Via Montenapoleone, in Milan's Golden Fashion Rectangle, and in the other in Galleri Vittorio Emanuele II, above the Prada menswear outfitters – each sporting a brighter version of Prada's signature crème de menthe. But we prefer the unsurpassable historic outpost with its original fittings, which Prada has sensibly left pretty much unchanged. Still managed by family scion Angelo Marchesi, the bar/café/pastry shop has a polished mahogany bar and glass-topped counters, vintage mirrors and art deco lamps.

Most clients – a mix of be-suited and bespectacled Milanese *signori*, young fashion types and well-dressed tourists – prop up the bar with an espresso or cappuccino and buttery house-baked brioche (morning), or a bright red Marchesi cocktail with Carpano vermouth, gin, Martini Bitter and a secret herbal concoction (aperitif hour). There's also a small *salotto*, with four tables and green velvet armchairs, for those who wish to sample Marchesi's pasticcini (dainty cakes including miniature chocolate rings with raspberries, and tiny custard flans topped with strawberries) with a cup of sustainable forest grown Thai tea. There are also beautifully wrapped packets of pink or lilac sugared almonds, chocolate dragees and gumdrops arranged like Gerhard Richter colour charts. But best of all are the paper-wrapped sourdough panettoni, the airy Christmas cakes with dry raisins and candied peel, said to be invented in fifteenth-century Milan by a kitchen lad named Toni – hence 'Tony's bread', or 'pane di Toni' – and available at Marchesi all year. Like all things Prada, prices aren't for the faint-hearted, but this is a quintessential slice of Milan ○

La Marquise

Zagreb, Croatia

Rebar ulica 25, 10000
Zagreb, Croatia
+385 95 770 3419

The chocolate and raspberry
Valentine's Day cake sports
a devil and a heart.

The tale of La Marquise is, at heart, a love story. Croatian Sebastien Vermant and his wife, Frenchwoman Céline, met as teenagers and travelled the world, before settling in Slovenia. On their frequent visits to Zagreb, just over the border, they realised that the city's bakery scene needed livening up, and a plan was hatched to open a French-style patisserie and boulangerie. Sebastien went to France to study pastry-making, baking and chocolate craftsmanship; Céline worked on developing a brand. The pair hired and trained other bakers and cake-makers, sourced French suppliers and producers, and in 2017 opened a modest outlet in Zagreb's hilly reaches, close to the city's French school.

Interior decoration was kept to a minimum, but the pair went to town on the baked goods. The display cabinet – which stretches the length of the shop – was filled with eclairs, croissants, tarts, macarons, brioches, biscuits, cakes and pastries. A range of rustic loaves was stacked up behind. Word of mouth spread fast and La Marquise soon developed a following. New offerings, such as tarte Tropézienne (a cream-filled brioche) and Paris-Brest (choux pastry and praline flavoured cream), helped maintain their fan base.

Once the shop was firmly established, even more varied items debuted: bread with cheddar cheese, beer and ham, or figs and museli; orange-chocolate and almond croquante; apricot and honey bread; basil and lemon macarons. Now they also supply various restaurants, and offer cakes to order for birthdays and other special events, such as the chocolate and raspberry Valentine's Day cake which sports a devil and a heart. Today, La Marquise has a larger outlet at Bukovačka 25, and there are plans for one near Bundek park and another in town at Petrinjska ⊙

McKee's Country Store and Restaurant

Newtownards,
Northern Ireland

Strangford View Farm,
28 Holywood Road,
Newtownards, BT23 4TQ,
Northern Ireland
mckeesproduce.com

Chunks of homemade bread, lavish cakes and enormous signature scones.

McKee's is an award-winning, family run business, tucked into the lush Craigantlet hills outside Belfast, not far from Newtownards. The McKees have farmed this rich County Down land since 1922. All the pies, pasties and baked goods in the deli, all the meat in the butcher's, and everything served in the restaurant is prepared on the premises, and most of it comes from the surrounding fields. The journey from field to plate is reassuringly short – the clucking hens you see from the car park, for example, lay eggs that are whisked into the giant pavlovas served in the restaurant.

The dining rooms are big, bright and noisy. The menu is similarly no nonsense, with unfussy comfort food in the form of hearty breakfasts, big bowls of soup with even bigger chunks of homemade bread, lavish cakes and enormous signature scones. These come plain or in a variety of flavours – fruit or cherry, rhubarb and ginger, raspberry and white chocolate, apple and cinnamon, date and wheaten. These generous slabs, served warm with homemade jams, are a meal in themselves. The fruit-filled tarts and crumbles and fluffy pancakes also go some way to explain why there is rarely an empty seat in the place. A full range of baked goods is available from the store, where the bakery produces wheaten, soda and potato breads, biscuits, apple pies, chocolate cakes, butterfly buns, tray bakes and much, much more.

There is something quintessentially Northern Irish about McKee's. What it might lack in elegance or fashion, it compensates for with a lack of pretentiousness and a dedication to quality. In other words, what it does, it does very well indeed ◦

Meyers Bakery

Copenhagen, Denmark

♀ Jægersborggade 9, 2200
Copenhagen, Denmark
↟ meyersmad.dk

The cinnamon twirls, made from a rich dough containing plenty of organic Danish butter.

Jægersborggade's transformation from a rather shady street to a trendy hangout is pretty much complete. These days the road, in the city's up-and-coming Nørrebro neighbourhood, is lined with cool cafés and chic boutiques and is an appropriate setting for the best-loved (and first) of the four bakeries in the Meyers Group. Claus Meyer, who established the group, is a well-known chef and entrepreneur who played a big part in the New Nordic Cuisine movement (he co-founded Noma in 2003).

Meyers bakes only with organic flour grown in the Nordic region, favouring wholegrain and using sourdough in all its pastries and breads. The firm has developed a baking technique which involves using a large amount of water in the dough, cold-rising the dough over a minimum of twelve hours and then baking it at a very high temperature.

The result is an aromatic moist bread with a dark and crispy crust. The signature Oland wheat bread, for example, uses a grain with a high protein and gluten content that gives a good flavour and has fine baking qualities. Other breads include rye loaves, baguettes and a variety of rolls. Baking is something everyone can relate to, says Kristina Sandager of Meyers: 'We have a broad crowd of regular customers who share our basic philosophy of ecology and good craftmanship.'

The sweet stuff is carefully crafted too. The vanilla cream and the jam used in the pastries are made in house, and a lot of time is spent refining and developing recipes. The cinnamon twirls, made from a rich dough containing plenty of organic Danish butter, are particularly popular, but there are croissants, pains au chocolat, buns and scones as well. The bakery gives away portions of sourdough starter (for free, bring your own container), and also sells flour, grains, own-made apple juice and cookery books ○

Moser's Backparadies

Baden, Switzerland

◉ Schlossbergplatz 2, 5400 Baden, Switzerland

⚲ backparadies.ch/ baeckerei

Spanischbrödli, a delicious if rather dumpy looking square of crisp butter pastry with hazelnut and apricot jam.

There's a cool story attached to the bakeries of Baden, which revolves around a local delicacy called Spanischbrödli, a delicious if rather dumpy looking square of crisp butter pastry with hazelnut and apricot jam. (These days, the fillings include carrot and hazelnut, and savoury ones with carrot and ham.) Back in the eighteenth and nineteenth centuries, the original version of this popular treat was banned from sale in nearby Zwinglian Zurich, so the Zurich aristocracy would send their servants overnight on foot to bring the brödli back fresh in the morning, tramping twenty-five kilometres to make the delivery. The ability to offer Spanischbrödli to guests for breakfast was a sign of prestige.

Nowadays, you can get from Zurich to Baden in fifteen minutes by train (in fact, the train has been colloquially known as the *Spanisch-Brötli-Bahn* since it opened in 1847 – Switzerland's first railway line) and enjoy one of these historic treats at any time. Probably the best place in which to do so is at Moser's Backparadies.

Moser's is a large, airy bakery and café in the centre of Baden, set on a cobblestoned square complete with Baroque fountains. Besides the Spanischbrödli and a cast of the usual Swiss-bakery sweets (Cremeschnitte, Schoggibrötli and the like), Moser's also offers an innovative selection of Berliners – a Swiss-German favourite that is basically a jam doughnut. They're not the greasy showground variety though, but rather a cloud of light, sweet pastry surrounding a heart of tasty, tart, jewel-toned conserve. The Berliners here also come spilling open with vanilla or lemon-kokos (lemon-coconut) cream or covered in sparkly pink rhubarb sugar.

Another local delicacy is Badener Stein, sold by the box – not stones, but cubes of chocolate with a hazelnut, biscuit and cherry filling.

Moser's also carries a good selection of Swiss breads – the humble Hausbrot, the huge, flat Badener Wannenbrot, the craggy St Gallerbrot, and the shiny plaited Zopf – and other bread varieties containing nuts, pumpkin and potato. There's also a range of house-made quiches and sandwiches available.

The nicest time to visit is on a Saturday. This is market day in central Baden, with stalls selling fresh produce and flowers. Take a seat and kick back with a coffee, the newspapers and a brödli ⊙

Namur

Luxembourg

♀ 27 rue des Capucins,
L-1313 Luxembourg
♠ namur.lu

One of the rare patisseries that makes its crème de marrons from scratch, using chestnuts from Turin.

One of Luxembourg's oldest patisseries, Namur dates back to 1863 and has long since been a *fournisseur de la cour* (an official supplier of Luxembourg's royal palace). This renowned institution is still a family business and is now into its sixth generation. The grand, old-school charm of its flagship store in the centre of Luxembourg City attracts a mix of Luxembourg seniors and tourists, who mostly come here for a coffee and patisserie or ice cream. Mirrored wood-panelled rooms, marble flooring and art deco details set the scene for a wealth of counters displaying chocolates, confections and cakes, all made with the finest ingredients: Sicilian almonds, untreated Spanish oranges, hazelnuts from Piedmont . . . The results are near perfect, and include textbook examples of raspberry frangipane tartlets and eclairs.

The larger dessert cakes always draw a crowd; they're usually pre-ordered as the pièce de résistance at Luxembourg dinner parties. Namur prides itself on being one of the rare patisseries that makes its crème de marrons from scratch, using chestnuts from Turin. This excellent chestnut purée is best sampled in their celebrated mont blanc (a mountain-shaped tartelette of whipped cream topped with chestnut purée). Savoury dishes – sandwiches, salads and quiches – are also served in the café and on the terrace.

For a little something to savour later, Namur's delicate chocolates are a winning option. Made in small batches, they come filled with the likes of homemade marzipan, almond croquant and ganache, and most of them are made to century-old recipes. But for a truly local specialty, opt for a bag of Bamkuchspitz. For this twist on a classic, Namur has cut Luxembourg's famed layer cake, the Bamkuch, into little nuggets and dipped them in chocolate, to delightful effect ◉

Oberweis

Luxembourg

📍 16 Grand Rue, L-1660
Luxembourg

🔖 oberweis.lu

The firm has links with Japan and takes inspiration from regular exchanges with Japanese pastry chefs.

Less traditional than its counterpart Namur, Oberweis is constantly innovating its sweet and savoury repertoire. People flock here for the superb miniature cakes, which can be enjoyed in the tearoom upstairs or on the terrace out front. This sleek, modern flagship store on the pedestrian Grand Rue is the subject of some controversy – the recent move from their traditional shop just opposite upset some conservative *Luxembourgers*. At Oberweis, classics such as custard-filled mille feuilles or coffee eclairs are rivalled by a constantly changing range of novelties. Take the piña colada savarin: an almond sponge topped with rum-vanilla cream, pineapple juice-soaked savarin and served with a piña colada cocktail pipette. Or the chocolate jalousie: a hazelnut praline topped with three layers of dark, milk and white chocolate mousse.

The firm has links with Japan and takes inspiration from regular exchanges with Japanese pastry chefs. The result is a cutesy aesthetic and Japanese flavours such as yuzu and matcha finding their way into Oberweis's French-style patisserie and macarons. Indeed, Oberweis is said to make the best macarons in Luxembourg, with a range that runs from classic flavours to seasonal specials such as lychee or speculoos. They're also famed for their chocolate truffles, as befits a *fournisseur de la cour* (official supplier of Luxembourg's royal Palace), and the chocolatiers put great emphasis on sourcing the right cocoa beans. The most iconic sweet treat here, however, is the mini Bamkuch, Luxembourg's tree-trunk-shaped layer cake ⦾

Old Post Office Bakery

London, England

⦿ 76 Landor Road, London SW9 9PH, England
⚲ oldpostofficebakery.co.uk

Lemon and poppyseed and pineapple upside-down cakes look almost too good to eat.

London's oldest organic bakery is still keeping the faith in unassuming premises in Clapham, and will bring a warm glow to those with fond memories of twentieth-century co-operatives and community activism. Karl Heinz Rossbach started baking in 1982 after he moved to London from Germany and couldn't find a decent loaf. At the time, he was living in a squatted ex-post office, and so the Old Post Office bakery was born. Current owners John Dungavel and Richard Scroggs joined him a few years later, and all three share the same inclusive ideals and a belief in keeping the bakery small enough so that it can remain properly artisan. This doesn't mean the results are dull or worthy – just check out the range of cakes. Lemon and poppyseed and pineapple upside-down cakes look almost too good to eat, and the lush chocolate cake belies its vegan tag; the

Chelsea bun is less pretty but is a blissfully doughy mouthful.

There's very little space, but a lot is packed in. The bakery is at the back; in the shop at the front there's a small counter laden with cakes and buns, a windowful of bread and yet more tin loaves neatly stacked on shelves behind the counter. These come in small sizes (no more wasted bread) as well as large, and are keenly priced (another example of the community-minded ethos). The range is impressive, from white tin loaves and bloomers perfect for sandwiches, to an assortment of sourdoughs. There are various rye breads, including the delicious Holsteiner (100 per cent stone-ground rye flour, whole rye grains, sunflower seeds, molasses, oats, salt and water), plus seeded loaves, spelt bread, malted grain and fruit loaves.

Bakers from all over the world have passed through the bakery, so as well as

traditional British items (Victoria sponges, Eccles cakes, fruit scones, pasties) there are excellent fruit-stuffed Danish pastries, pain aux raisins, focaccia and the like.

There's no room to eat in, but there's a brisk trade in take-away lunch items: filled bread rolls, warm cheese and onion pasties, chunks of leek and potato pie, big slices of pizza and spinach and feta rolls. The Old Post Office Bakery's bread and cakes can also be found at several farmers' markets, including ones in central London (Bloomsbury and Marylebone) ⦿

Olof Viktors Bageri och Café

Glemmingebro, Sweden

📍 Österlenvägen 86, 271 75 Glemmingebro, Sweden
🔗 olofviktors.se

On a sunny day, head for a table in the cobbled courtyard or the apple orchard.

Going for a 'fika-excursion' is something of a national pastime in Sweden (at least in the summer), where rural cafés dot the countryside. The immensely popular Olof Viktors gives you a chance to enjoy fika in a cosy environment in Österlen ('the Tuscany of Skåne') all year round. On a sunny day, head for a table in the cobbled courtyard or the apple orchard; if the weather is poor, find a charming nook in the old farmhouse where the café/bakery is situated.

Olof Viktors was started by the renowned Jan Hedh, the grand old man of the Swedish pastry world and the author of many popular cookbooks on everything from ice cream to pralines. He was also one of the first sourdough advocates in Sweden, long before it became fashionable, and all the bread here is slow risen, and baked in the large wood-fired oven. Keep an eye out for the traditional

Skanian kavring, a heavy, slightly sweet rye bread that goes well with local herring; the crispbread is good, too. You can of course buy a whole loaf, but there are also delicious Danish-style open sandwiches on offer. Locally sourced toppings include cheese from the nearby Vilhelmsdal dairy and shrimp with fresh peas and bleak roe.

All the classic Swedish cakes are here, as well as some more modern innovations. The fantastically intense chocolate ball and the caramel pecan brownie are both highly recommended, as are the luscious beetroot cake and the liquorice cream bun. In the summer months, homemade ice cream is offered – just one of the many reasons children love the place. Coffee comes from the small local roaster Lilla Kafferosteriet in Skåne, and is lovingly prepared ⊙

Padaria Ribeiro

Porto, Portugal

♀ Praça Guilherme Gomes
Fernandes 21-27, 4050-
294 Porto, Portugal
↟ padariaribeiro.com

It's pick 'n' mix for gourmands.

Padaria means bread bakery, and Padaria Ribeiro has been peddling loaves for over 140 years. There are now five branches, but the original still stands in the tranquil edge of Porto's pretty centre, on Praça Guilherme Gomes Fernandes. In the nineteenth century, it was referred to as *Praça do Pão* – bread square – thanks to the regular markets held here. These days it's the perfect spot to watch the world go by while devouring goodies from this local institution. Opt for a take-away and sit on a bench in the sun: staff at the counter are marvellously efficient, but service in the café is desultory.

Like a display in a candy shop, dozens of bread roll varieties (each kept crusty in its own perspex drawer) make a checkerboard wall behind the glass counter, under which there are perfect little piles of cakes, biscuits and tarts. Join the queue, full of locals buying fresh loaves for the next family meal, for specialities such as broa de Avintes, a heavy, sticky, rye-based loaf, or for the ubiquitous white dinner rolls (carcaças), soft and light as cotton wool inside but with a thin, crisp, golden crust – thanks in part to the fact that here they're stone-baked. Make sure you also order the rissóis de camarão, a dinky pastry package stuffed with prawns that resembles a Findus crispy pancake.

Although this is a padaria – rather than a pastelaria (pastry shop) – save space for the sweet treats too. Pack a selection box with whatever you fancy, but do include a few tartes de amêndoa, topped with crunchy slivers of toasted almond flakes in a gently chewy and delightfully buttery caramel. There are exemplary pasteis de nata, of course, but it's worth choosing a few wildcards from the array. You pay by weight, so just pile them in – it's pick 'n' mix for gourmands ◦

Panella Roma

Rome, Italy

⚲ Via Merulana 54, 00185
   Rome, Italy
⚓ panellaroma.com

Maria Grazia Panella has artfully blended traditional Roman techniques and ingredients with a modern sensibility.

Opened in 1929 by Augusto Panella, Panella Roma is centrally located, a ten minute walk from the Coliseum. It's on a pleasant piazza, in an area stuffed full of bakeries and pizzerias. Panella Roma stands out though, partly for its legendary *antico forno* (ancient oven), but mostly due to the efforts of Maria Grazia Panella, who has owned and run the bakery since 1970, and has artfully blended traditional Roman techniques and ingredients with a modern sensibility.

Inside you'll find the bakery section to the left, with up to seventy varieties of bread, grissini and rolls. Around the walls of the area to the right are shelves of tempting goods in boxes, tins, packets and jars: tea, jam, locally milled flour, sardines, sweets, oils and spices. In the centre is a table heaving with food (antipasti, frittata, omelette, pizza, salads) set out for the evening buffet – best enjoyed with an Aperol spritz or prosecco at one of the tables outside on the piazza.

Shop assistants in floppy maroon baker's caps bustle about, serving customers with bread, pizza by the centimetre and sweet treats displayed under glass and in pallets (signs warn: 'no self service!'). The pastries are many and varied; from Hungarian cheese and cherry knots to chocolate brownies, strudels to Sachertorte, plus sweet and savoury croissants, tarts, cakes, brioche and, of course, tiramisu. In the morning, visitors can sample croissants stuffed with chocolate, cream or jam.

There are many loaves, of many nationalities. The sourdough is the most popular, though it's a close-run thing: asked what the bestseller was, an assistant pointed to the entire wall of bread. Italian varieties include Roman ciriola, Sicilian mafalda, Ferrarese crocetta and Cremonese bread, and there are multigrain loaves, nut breads and a gluten-free range too.

On a hot Roman evening, the lengths of flat pizza are irresistible. Choose a topping, browse the shop while the snack is warmed up, and then pick a scenic spot in which to enjoy some of the best pizza you've ever had ◦

Panificio Bonci

Rome, Italy

📍 Via Trionfale 36, Rome 00195, Italy
➤ bonci.it

Seven different types of natural yeast are combined with heritage grains to bake the fragrant, crusty loaves.

Tall, tattooed and talented, Gabriele Bonci has been known as the 'King of Pizza al Taglio' (Rome's famous pizza-by-the-slice) since soon after opening Pizzarium, a hole-in-the-wall take-out establishment near the Vatican, in 2003. Nine years later, he applied his encyclopaedic knowledge of grains, flours and yeasts to a bakery – Panificio Bonci – which opened close by, selling breads, cakes and biscuits alongside the pizza which made his name.

Since seating is extremely limited, smartly dressed Romans, workmen, students and tourists often gather beneath the bright blue 'Panificio' sign (which has become a local landmark), savouring their slices of crusty, airy pizza, while eyeing the toppings of fellow sybarites. A former TV chef, the Big Man himself is part of the attraction, but his carefully crafted dough and artisanal toppings are the main draw. Bonci uses

specially selected yeast and finely sifted Buratto Type 2 wheat flour (containing small quantities of fibre and wheat-germ) from artisanal Piedmontese miller Mulino Marino, whose flours are all organic and stone-milled. However, he famously claims that it is the *manipolazione*, or kneading, of the dough which gives it its light yet crispy quality. Depending on the season, his hundreds of toppings range from margherita, with basil from Bonci's herb garden, organic tomatoes from the Campania region and the best available buffalo mozzarella, to rich combinations such as (our favourite) caramelised peaches and porcini mushrooms.

Bonci's bread and baked goods display similar attention to detail. Seven different types of natural yeast are combined with heritage grains to bake the fragrant, crusty loaves stacked on shelves behind the glass counters. Among

the most popular are tangy spelt or rye loaves, again made with Mulino Marino's stone-milled organic flour, sacks of which you'll see in the shop. Cakes and biscuits are made with butter from Beppe e I Suoi Formaggi, the legendary Roman cheese shop, and give off tempting aromas of vanilla and bergamot. We love the lemony madeleines, the frothy coconut macaroons and, especially, the melt-in-the-mouth cornetti (croissants), made with aromatic spelt flour and Beppe's more-ish butter ○

Panificio Costantini

Venice, Italy

Via San Martino Sinistra 282, Burano, Venice 30142, Italy
+39 041 735595

The best biscotti are still made on the island.

The Venetian island of Burano is known for its bright red, yellow, green and blue fishermen's houses, and for its hand-made *punto in aria* (stitch in the air) needle lace. But it is also home to Venice's most famous biscuit, the bussolà. It's a large, ring-shaped biscuit, the colour of pale buttercups, made from flour, egg yolks, sugar and butter. Flavours include vanilla, lemon and rum. Rich, with a melt-in-the-mouth consistency, though drier and crumblier than shortbread, the bussola is originally said to have been prepared by fishermen's wives to provide long lasting energy while out at sea. The hole in the middle may have helped it to dry more efficiently, so that it remained crunchy and crisp in the middle of the Adriatic.

The best biscotti are still made on the island, and according to Venetians, the family-run Panificio Costantini is the prime place to snap them up.

In 2016, the shop was renovated: white-painted, glass-topped counters decorated with fashionable lettering give the interior a more modern look. But Costantini's baking methods are still rigorously authentic, based on a jealously guarded family recipe. The biscuits are hand-mixed, hand-shaped and placed on baking trays on oven-proof paper, before being cooked on the premises for fifteen minutes until they are slightly browned. Burano residents, Venetians from the main island (an hour-and-a-half away via two water buses) and tourists all queue alongside one another to pick up packets of biscuits.

Costantini also makes a variety of other Venetian specialties, including the esse, a smaller, S-shaped version of the bussola; zaletti (cornmeal biscuits with raisins or chocolate chips) and pevarini – spicy biscuits traditionally flavoured with white pepper. We recommend trying them all ○

Panificio Davide Longoni

Milan, Italy

📍 Via Tiraboschi 19, Milan 20135, Italy
🔗 davidelongonipane.com

The bestseller is the 'antique cereals', a round crusty loaf, incised with a circle, which mixes einkorn, rye, spelt and semi-wholegrain wheat.

The general consensus is that Davide Longoni's light and airy bakery-café, on a leafy street in the fashionable Porta Romana zone, sells the best bread in Milan. Seventy restaurants order their daily bread from Longoni, while the shop is patronised by well-heeled professionals in search of breakfast, lunch, aperitifs or one of the crusty heritage grain loaves. These are stacked on traditional wooden rods protruding from the wall behind the counter, and emit an alluring aroma. Each is carved with a different symbol denoting the grain from which the bread is made: a circle, a rhomboid, three lines, five slits, a series of dots.

The son of a baker from a village north of Milan, Longoni studied agriculture at university and became fascinated with heirloom grains – an interest he pursued when he followed in his father's footsteps around twenty years ago.

He found three small mills producing stone-ground flours: Mulinum di San Floro in Calabria, Mulino Sobrino in Piedmont and Molini del Ponte in Sicily. Each mill works with its own varieties of organic grains – from buckwheat in Piedmont to tumminia, a dark and flavoursome variety of durum wheat, in Sicily.

It is the stone-milling, Longoni believes, that accounts for his bread's exceptional aroma and taste: this traditional manner of milling means that grains don't overheat, so their essential character is preserved. The other vital component is, of course, the yeast. Longoni started up his *lievito madre* – literally 'mother yeast'– in 2003, and has nurtured this sourdough starter like a treasured pet ever since. As well as guaranteeing flavour, the *lievito madre* ensures longevity: wrapped in paper, most Longoni loaves will last for up to

three days, while rye loaves remain edible for around ten days, if treated properly.

Longoni's antique grain breads include farro, known in English as emmer or einkorn wheat. 'Farro monococco is the most antique cereal cultivated by man, the origin of all other cereals,' says Longoni. His farro loaves contain a mix of two kinds of einkorn wheat, plus spelt, which gives it a fresh, almost grassy flavour. Thanks to its low levels of gluten, it is also highly digestible.

But the bestseller is the 'antique cereals', a round crusty loaf, incised with a circle, which mixes einkorn, rye, spelt and semi-wholegrain wheat. Its complex flavour, which Longoni likens to a wine, has proved a hit with customers. At weekends, a constant stream of regulars come in for the Saturday special, challah, a plaited Jewish loaf. The dough contains a little honey, and its slightly sweet flavour

and soft consistency make it popular with children.

Other baked goodies run from focaccia and pizza with unusual toppings, to buckwheat and bilberry tarts; all of which can be devoured at café tables, or sitting on a bench flanking a vegetable and herb patch. Longoni recently opened a second shop at the Mercato del Suffragio, a covered market at Piazza Santa Maria del Suffragio ◦

Panificio Mario

Genoa, Italy

◆ Via San Vincenzo 61R,
  Genoa 16121, Italy
♪ panificiomario.it

The list of Mario's goodies runs to more than twenty types of focaccia and thirty kinds of bread.

If the number of locals tripping in and out of a bakery is a guarantee of authenticity, then Panificio Mario is as genuine as they come. Opened in 1939, and run by the Bargi family since 1969, the space, with its functionally tiled floor, overhead spotlights and steel-and-glass counters packed with baked goods, is nothing to write home about. Instead, it's all about the product: focaccia.

Genoa is the home of focaccia; the city's most famous singer-songwriter, Fabrizio De André, celebrated the 'perverse aroma of focaccia with onion'. That combo is still one of Mario's bestsellers, along with plain salted focaccia, focaccia with potato and rosemary, with tomato and oregano, with olives, with creamy Stracchino cheese, or, following a rare antique recipe, with flakes of dried sage. Even at the mid-point between breakfast and lunchtime, the place is packed with workmen in orange overalls, old ladies with walking frames, and mothers with toddlers and prams, all queuing for a take-away. Many people tuck in before they've left the premises, causing jams at the doors.

Genuine focaccia is a yeasted flatbread made with *strutto* or lard, explains Stefano Bargi, though in recent years, the bakery has also come up with a 'light focaccia', which is lard-free. Another specialty is focaccia Voltri, coated with a sprinkling of yellow polenta meal, whose crunchy texture contrasts beautifully with the springy bread below. Named after a district in West Genoa (Genova Ponente), 'it is cooked directly on the hotgrid, without a tin, on a layer of polenta meal,' says Stefano. Also from Genoa is farinata, a slim pancake, made with water, salt, chickpea flour and olive oil, whose rich, almost eggy flavour belies its healthy ingredient list. The list of Mario's goodies, posted on the wall, runs to more than twenty types of focaccia and thirty kinds of bread. If you can't decide, pop across the street to Panificio Mario Dolce Vita café to try some of the more intriguing specialities with a coffee, before choosing what to buy to take home ●

Parémi

Vienna, Austria

📍 Bäckerstraße 10, 1010
Vienna, Austria

🔗 paremi.at

A fresh batch of fougasse –
Provençal flatbread, here layered
with Roquefort cheese – emerging
from the traditional stone oven is
a particularly welcome sight.

There is no more suitable setting for a bakery in Austria than Bäckerstraße, where bread was baked in medieval Vienna. But Rémi Soulier and Patricia Petschenig's Parémi ('Pa-Rémi') is a very modern bakery, and a French one at that. It opened shortly before Christmas 2017, and customers flocked in from the beginning, attracted by Patricia's pralines, madeleines and macarons lined up behind the etched shop window (which reads 'Brioches, Pains au Chocolat, Croissants' in a classic French font).

Rémi (who trained at the renowned Ferrandi school in Paris) and his team of bakers take care of the breads, from sourdough baguettes to crusty rye loaves. All are top-notch, produced with flour from two small-scale mills, but a fresh batch of fougasse – Provençal flatbread, here layered with Roquefort cheese – emerging from the traditional stone oven is a particularly welcome sight.

Through a glass partition, the sweet stuff can be seen being hand-made; puff pastry and croissant dough are crafted into the likes of Brandteigkrapferl – a hazelnut-flavoured cream puff that's the house speciality. Even more elaborate is 'Le Citron', a delicate tart sold by the slice, in which lemon mousse brings out the white chocolate flavour.

Locals start the day here with freshly squeezed orange juice and a crunchy baguette slathered in homemade jam; later there are also quiches and salads. Add the lure of good coffee and the daily papers, and a light, airy, surprisingly spacious interior, and it's no wonder Parémi is busy ◦

Pariés

St-Jean-de-Luz, France

📍 9 rue Gambetta, 64500
St-Jean-de-Luz, France
🔖 paries.fr

It looks more like a jewellery shop than a bakery, with precious shiny packages tied with tangerine bows.

A classy bakery that's been in the same family for more than 100 years, Pariés' flagship sits on rue Gambetta, the main shopping street of Saint Jean de Luz. The shop is hard to miss with its cheery orange exterior: the signature colour was chosen as a way of injecting a little bit of sunshine into the rainy days common to the area. It looks more like a jewellery shop than a bakery, with precious shiny packages tied with tangerine bows and lines of chocolate displayed under glass cases. And they are precious – Pariés is focused on sourcing quality ingredients. The cocoa comes from Central American plantations, the hazelnuts from Piedmont in Italy and the cream from Normandy. All the confections – for all seven shops – used to be made in the workshop above this store, but since 2009 they come from a shiny workspace ten minutes outside of town.

The family started with chocolate, which was the specialty of the original shop (in Bayonne). Baked goods were not introduced until after World War I, and Pariés' crowning jewel, the gateau Basque, first appeared in the 1940s. This traditional gateau has a sable-like pastry sandwiching a thin filling of cherry preserve, and is a staple of the French Basque Country. Here, you can try an array of flavours: cherry, chocolate, orange-grapefruit and caramelised white chocolate with hazelnut. The bestseller comes stuffed with almond cream and there's even a gluten-free version.

In a region not known for innovative baking, Pariés stands out, thanks to five generations of chocolatiers and bakers having perfected their craft in different specialties and countries. One of the firm's most famous sweets is the mouchou, or 'the kiss' – two Italian-style meringues stuck together in the sweetest of kisses. The kanouga is the house's oldest product, a soft butter toffee that comes in an array of flavours, including one with a spicy kick from the local piment d'Espelette. The kanouga's curious name is a nod to the Russians who once came to nearby Biarritz in the summer – legend has it that Monsieur Pariés dropped his finger on a map of Russia and landed on the city of Kaluga. Another house speciality is the almond and sugar turron, which Pariés perfected after an extended sojourn in Toledo, Spain. Now the all-natural turrons come in a variety of flavours; one even sports the design of the Basque *ikurriña* flag ●

Pastas Beatriz

Pamplona, Spain

Calle de la Estafeta 22, 31001 Pamplona, Spain
+34 948 22 06 18

A batch right out of the oven is a revelation – impossibly buttery, overstuffed with chocolate, and a perfect balance between crunchy and soft.

It is easier to find Pastas Beatriz by smell than by sight. The tiny storefront on Calle Estafeta in Pamplona's old town is nothing more than a window, a door and a bit of peeling brown trim. The aroma wafting down the street, however, is pure heaven: the smell of butter melting between layers of puff pastry and chocolate oozing onto a hot baking tray.

This smell floats out as tray after tray of the bakery's famous garroticos are carried out to the shopfront from the bakery in the back. They are the signature pastry of this tiny, family-owned shop. The founder Lourdes Gomez and her sister Asunción still operate the mixer and the ovens, arriving at 3am each morning to prepare the famous chocolate pastries, whose name means 'little baton'. A batch right out of the oven is a revelation – impossibly buttery, overstuffed with chocolate, and a perfect balance between crunchy and soft.

Lourdes Gomez took the shop over from the previous owners (who ran it as more of a general store), and they passed on many of their recipes. Now there's a wall of wooden boxes stuffed with over a dozen different traditional tea biscuits, or pastas. You can have coconut macaroons, with and without chocolate; biscuits made with lard, with and without almond; peanut cookies; biscuits sandwiched with chocolate or filled with raspberry or apricot; tiny ones topped with a maraschino cherry; rosquilla, or anise fritters, and various others. A stream of customers walk out with a box packed with a variety selection, weighed and priced by the kilo, often by Lourdes's son, Jon.

It's not all pastas, though. The shop window displays piles of simple baked goods: muffins with and without chocolate, palmiers (plain and filled with white chocolate and hazelnut), yoghurt cake and puff pastry creations. Pastas Beatriz sells one of the best walnut cakes for miles around – moist and tasting of fresh walnuts. That so many cakes and biscuits can come out of such a tiny space is a testament to the passion and skill of its owners ○

Pastéis de Belém

Lisbon, Portugal

⚲ Rua Belém 84–92, 1300–085 Lisbon, Portugal
⚑ pasteisdebelem.pt

The hand-made tarts are melt-in-your-mouth buttery, with crisp, ultra-thin layers of pastry, scorched caramelised tops and the creamiest custard fillings.

Pastéis de Belém – also known as Antiga Confeitaria de Belém – is on every tourist's itinerary in ever-popular Lisbon; you won't find a guidebook that doesn't include it in its shortlist of 'must-dos'. The pasteleria's popularity is based not only on its exemplary custard tarts – though their deliciousness cannot be denied – but also on its history. For Pastéis de Belém is in possession of the original pastel de nata (Portuguese custard tart) recipe – a still-secret concoction of eggs, cream, sugar, cinnamon and flaky pastry, the exact quantities of which are only known by an ultra-select group of master bakers.

The story goes that the recipe for the tarts originated from the monks of the spectacular Mosteiro dos Jerónimos, a pastel's throw away, which sat next to a sugarcane refinery. When the monastery was shut down in 1834, the family who owned the refinery bought the secret recipe from the monks and then opened the Fábrica de Pastéis de Belém shortly after, in 1837. The descendants of the original family still use the closely guarded (now, in fact, patented) recipe to this day.

So, are the tarts noticeably different to others you'll find all around Lisbon? You won't be disappointed. The hand-made tarts are melt-in-your-mouth buttery, with crisp, ultra-thin layers of pastry, scorched caramelised tops and the creamiest custard fillings. They are this bakery's raison d'être, its razão de ser, so every step is taken to ensure that each one of the 30,000 or so made each day is perfect. Many Lisboetas say that Manteigaria's slightly saltier pasteis now have the edge, but only the most discerning of custard tart eaters will notice any difference. These are custard tarts par excellence. Served warm,

with or without extra cinnamon, they are among Portugal's finest culinary offerings. You can order other sweet Portuguese delicacies here but, really, why would you want to?

Of course, the bakery being in every guidebook means that you'll be sharing your custard tart experience with hordes of tourists, especially in peak season. In fact, the take-away queue for Pastéis de Belém is these days something of a barometer for how touristy Lisbon is as a whole at any time of year – especially as the bakery is open 352 days a year. It's bafflingly easy to avoid the queue, however, by simply choosing to eat inside the cavernous café. Even if you want to buy tarts to take away, in the beautifully designed blue and white cardboard tubes, it's still much easier and quicker to do it via this route. Once inside, choose either the windowless, slightly soulless room in

the middle – which does however have views of the bakers at work – or the larger, more decorative back room with traditional tiling and an adjoining courtyard ◦

Pastelería Arrese

Bilbao, Spain

⦿ Gran Vía 24, 48001
Bilbao, Spain
⚲ arrese.biz

Arrese's bestseller is the chocolate-coated palmier, a lovely, thick, elephant-eared puff pastry, dipped in a generous bath of chocolate.

The grand dame of Bilbao bakeries, with six shops across the greater metropolitan area, Pastelería Arrese was founded in 1852. The oldest operating branch is this one, with a regal storefront on central shopping thoroughfare Gran Vía. This emblematic shop opened its doors in 1923 and the décor reflects a golden era: luxurious marble countertops, meticulously carved wooden shelving and grand high ceilings (and was, until the 1980s, the site of the bakery as well). One look at the perfectly aligned pastries rolled out on carts, however, and it's clear that the golden days are far from over.

Josetxu, the sixth generation of Arrese bakers, is bright-eyed with ideas for the bakery's future. 'I don't want to just live off the interest,' he says. He oversees a team that looks for constant improvements (perfecting the puff pastry, sourcing local butter from a small producer), and new creations, like the croissants stuffed with pistachio paste or wrapped around dark chocolate and candied orange. Arrese's bestseller is the chocolate-coated palmier, a lovely, thick, elephant-eared puff pastry, dipped in a generous bath of chocolate. On a busy shopping day, this shop can sell more than a thousand. On the shelves, the palmiers sit next to a line-up of classic Basque pastries – pastel ruso, a popular meringue layered dessert; pastel de arroz, a custard tart famous in Bilbao; carolinas, with their dainty meringue cap; gateau Basque; Santiago tarts (a Galician almond paste tart, dusted with icing sugar and adorned with the cross of Santiago) – plum cakes, apple tarts, muffins and more.

Funnily enough, though, if you ask any *Bilbaíno* what Arrese brings to mind, they will say 'truffles'. Arrese's plastic wrapped truffles are famous across Basque Country, and are notable for their size. These are no delicate, perfectly shaped bonbons – Arrese truffles are large, irregularly formed, and the only ornamentation is a dusting of confectioner's sugar (to identify the different flavours, from classic plain chocolate to Cointreau). No local get-together is complete without them ⊙

Pastelería Oiartzun

San Sebastián, Spain

📍 Calle de Igentea 2, 20003 San Sebastián, Spain

↖ pasteleriaoiartzun.com

All the greatest hits of Basque Country baking are here.

Resplendent on the corner of San Sebastián's main boulevard, Pastelería Oiartzun looks like it's been there for centuries, although it only arrived in 1988. The bakery started out in 1972, in a nearby village by the same name. Owner Manolo Martín slowly edged closer and closer to the capital, until he and his son David were installed in this prime spot.

The shop's decoration may not have changed much since the opening, with its chandeliers and crown moulding, but the sweets are on constant rotation. All the greatest hits of Basque Country baking are here: goxua, the Basque nod to tiramisu; cocos, like coconut macaroons; gateau Basque; pastel ruso (a layered meringue); the vintage triángulo de chocolate 'chocolate triangle', a layered chocolate cake, and dozens more on any given day. There are also croissants, and a lovely 'brioche', which in this case is croissant dough with a bit of added sweetness, studded with raisins. It typically sells out, so get here in the morning, when it's served warm off the top of the espresso machine.

The big sellers are the roca, which sit in piles of milk and dark chocolate in the bakery window. A popular local treat, it gets the name from its rock-like shape. Usually made of pieces of nut heaped and drenched in chocolate, Oiartzun's version is made of broken ice cream wafers. Once a neat way of using surplus ingredients, nowadays the delicacy is such a hit that extra wafers are needed to make them.

The Oiartzun ice cream parlour is next door to the pastry shop, and is one of the best in the city. The ice creams, made on-site using 100 natural ingredients, come in many flavours, from chocolate or mango to leche merengada, a cinnamon milk creation ◦

Patisserie Holtkamp

Amsterdam, Netherlands

⚲ Vijzelgracht 15, 1017 HM
Amsterdam, Netherlands
🔖 patisserieholtkamp.nl

A sophisticated aesthetic
and sensory delight.

Holtkamp is a patisserie of grown-up dreams, a sophisticated aesthetic and sensory delight from start to finish. The pleasure starts as soon as you set eyes on the wood-panelled exterior of this architectural gem on Vijzelgracht street, in the central canal district. Elaborate window displays of tempting treats entice passers-by, while loyal regulars are prepared to join the queue down the street on busy Saturday mornings, as they know the unsurpassed quality of the goods inside (as do the Dutch royals: Holtkamp is an official supplier).

Cees Holtkamp and his wife Petra started their confectionary business here in 1969, but the shop itself dates back further, to 1928. Designed by architect Piet Kramer (one of the most important architects of the Amsterdam School) for the owner of a pastry business that came before, the compact interior – which only fits eight or so customers at a time – is pure art deco, with rosewood walls, geometric stained glass door panels and original patterned murals on the upper reaches of the walls. Angela Holtkamp (daughter of Cees) took over the reins with husband Nico in 2002, and instigated a decade-long restoration; today the shop looks spectacular.

Patisserie Holtkamp's baked goods are made in the much larger bakery space downstairs and to the rear. The macaroons, cakes, tarts and chocolates on display are all fittingly elaborate. Patisserie classics in the glass fridge counter, such as classic Dutch tompouce – cream-filled pastry slices – and French opera cakes, compete for attention with more homely numbers, such as boterkoek (butter and almond cake) and citroentaart. The hand-made chocolates are especially impressive, with many incorporating aspects of the shop – for instance, the decoration of the 'tableau' chocolate slices reflects the shop's beautiful floor tiles (which in turn echo Piet Mondrian's work of the same name), while the Petra and Angela chocolates are named after family members. Elegant wall cabinets are lined with the likes of arnhemse meisjes (Dutch sugar cookies) and frisian dumkes (hazelnut and aniseed biscuits) in beautiful packaging stamped with the Futurist Holtkamp logo. This is also the place to visit if you're looking for a special occasion cake of the richly indulgent cream and fresh fruit variety.

And if you don't have a sweet tooth? Don't let that put you off, as Holtkamp is also, somewhat surprisingly, celebrated for its savoury kroketten (croquettes) – the prawn version is the house speciality ○

Patisserie Sainte Anne

London, England

● 204 King Street, London W6 0RA, England
▸ patisseriesainteanne.co.uk

All the French patisserie favourites are here, including some with a Japanese accent.

The pink exterior of Patisserie Sainte Anne reflects the colours of the picture-perfect gateaux sold inside. The yellow and pink interior is equally vibrant, and it's the ideal antidote to a wet English day – choose from the range of specialist teas, settle back with a pretty tarte aux pommes or a deliciously doughy kouign amann, and all's right with the world. Unlikely as it sounds, Patisserie Sainte Anne moved from the 13th arrondissement in Paris to Ravenscourt Park in west London in 2014, and is now firmly embedded in the neighbourhood. There's a sizeable local French community, and the friendly staff switch between French and English with ease; they are also endlessly patient with customers who agonise over which treat to order.

Everything – the cakes, the pastries, the bread and the chocolates – is made on the premises. It's hard to imagine, as there's not much space, with the little café area tucked around the sweep of the glass display cabinet. All the French patisserie favourites are here, including some with a Japanese accent. Many of them are gluten-free, such as the vivid green Hokusai, made of pear mousse, chestnut cream and green tea biscuit. There are large tarts and cakes, as well as individual ones, and festive cakes on special occasions, such as bûche de Noël (chocolate yule log) and galette des roi (traditionally served at Epiphany). Equally showstopping are the chocolates, in flavours such as crispy matcha and dark chocolate with yuzu, or whole cherries, soaked in sloe gin then dipped in chocolate. Most photogenic are the chocolate figures, some praline filled. Children tend to linger longest at this cabinet, gazing at orange squirrels and green dinosaurs, and Santas and Easter eggs in season. Macarons come in a choice of colours and flavours: yuzu, matcha, raspberry, salted caramel and more.

The small selection of French breads, all made with organic flour, includes wholemeal loaves and baguettes. A host of baked goods like palmiers, canelé, individual brioche, chouquettes, pain aux raisins and many more sit next to the till. There are a few savoury items – lunch rolls, tartiflette and deep-filled quiches – but really Patisserie Sainte Anne is a temple to the sweet things in life ●

Patisserie Tarte & Törtchen

Stuttgart, Germany

📍 Gutbrodstraße1, 70197 Stuttgart, Germany
🖈 tarteundtoertchen.de

Sweet cinnamon Franzbrötchen are an afternoon favourite.

This charming patisserie-cum-café is a real treat. Located in a lovely old building in the west of Stuttgart, Tarte & Törtchen is a welcoming spot filled with wooden furniture and mismatched crockery. It has a certain French flair, thanks to the chalkboards and gold-framed pictures on the walls above the gorgeous glass pastry counter. The café is almost always busy; in summer, take advantage of the wooden tables out front.

The café is open for breakfast, lunch, and afternoon treats. Enjoy a leisurely breakfast of good coffee alongside croissants and homemade jam, or a classic German tiered spread of bread rolls with cheese, a boiled egg, a bowl of seasonal fruit salad and a tiny cake. The quiches, which include vegetarian options, are popular at lunchtime. Sweet cinnamon Franzbrötchen are an afternoon favourite, and in summer there's ice cream, too. However, it's the exquisite tortes that really draws people here.

Hand-made by the patisserie's confectionary team and carefully positioned on porcelain stands on the glass counter, the neat line of striking, creatively decorated tortes almost look too good to eat. They're every bit as delicious as they look, from the Wunderland – a polka-dot poppyseed mousse with white chocolate that's covered in a dark purple layer of blackcurrant – to Himbeere á la Provence, a fruity raspberry cream with a lemon yoghurt base. If you really can't decide, try the Midnight, a crunchy, caramelised nut coated with a delicious espresso vanilla cream and topped with a white chocolate sail.

From the quality breads and rolls to the splendid tarts, nothing is made with artificial flavours or preservatives; all the suppliers (usually organic, Fairtrade or regional) are listed on a chalkboard. It all makes for brisk trade, so get there early if you've set your heart on something in particular as many items sell out ○

Pékműhely

Budapest, Hungary

Batthyány utca 24, 1015
Budapest, Hungary

pekmuhely.hu

Pékműhely translates
as 'Baker's Workshop'.

Pékműhely is the living embodiment of one man's mission to bring sourdough to Budapest. József Vajda had no connection with the baking trade, but had travelled enough around Europe to take a liking to slow fermented bread. 'I grew up with mass-produced loaves,' he remembers. 'When I discovered sourdough in Germany, I wanted to buy some here. I even put out an ad. Several bakers replied but said that this kind of bread simply didn't exist. In fact, couldn't exist.' To prove them wrong, Vajda went to several workshops abroad – Pékműhely translates as 'Baker's Workshop' – and began to try his hand at making it. When it came to selling his sourdough, local bakeries weren't interested in this exotic, un-oblong curiosity. So he decided to set up on his own.

Halfway up Batthyány utca, this original branch of Pékműhely remains a rustic-looking hive of activity. There's room for an oven, a counter, three wooden shelves of enticing artisanal breads, a display of pastries and a solitary table. A long, low wall outside doubles up as a communal resting spot. There's no price list, so your server, perhaps Vajda's wife Kata, will talk you through the three sourdough varieties on offer that day. If your Hungarian vocabulary doesn't stretch as far as szárított paradicsom (sun-dried tomatoes), one of the regulars in the queue will put you straight. Kovászos kenyér is sourdough bread. There will also be tönköly (spelt) available. Usually Kata or her colleague will slice off a small chunk for you to try, if the loaf is deemed cool enough. By late afternoon, the· customer base halves in age as parents make good on the promise of a kakáos csiga (cocoa spiral, or snail) on the way home from school.

Now with three outlets and a staff of thirty, Vajda still decries the quality of Hungarian flour and grain, feeling the domestic industry is still geared towards speed and yeast. 'Bread isn't there to bulk you out,' he concludes. 'It's there for your health.' Hence his new venture: a school for sourdough bakers ●

Pelivan

Belgrade, Serbia

♀ Bulevar kralja Aleksandra
20, 11000 Belgrade, Serbia
♪ pelivanbeograd.rs

This being Belgrade, the influences don't just come from Istanbul but Vienna, too.

Today, Pelivan sits at a busy Belgrade crossroads, right opposite the imposing main national post office. In 1851, when Mustafa Pelivanović started serving cakes and sweets of Ottoman and Habsburg heritage, stamps hadn't yet come to Serbia. Since then, both this charmingly traditional *poslasticarnica* (patisserie) and Belgrade have lived through every kind of upheaval the Balkans can throw at them.

Both have somehow survived, though the blitz of 6 April 1941 destroyed the original Pelivan by Belgrade Fortress's Stamboul Gate. Months later, it relocated here, to the main thoroughfare locals call 'Bulevar'. It's still very much a locals' place, just off the tourist radar, and identifiable by an old-school awning with gorgeous joined-up Cyrillic writing. Inside, the cumbersome cast-iron chairs, marble-topped tables and sepia prints of old Belgrade give the impression that some things never change.

Certainly, Pelivan hasn't lost touch with its Ottoman roots. There's baklava, but there's also kadayif – of the same family, and here made with walnuts, butter and sugar (rather than honey). Tulumba, the stunted cousin of the Spanish churros, is another sweetmeat that survives from the early days. The café still sells calorie-rich boza, an acidic sweet drink made from corn and yeast, brought over by the Turks centuries ago.

But this being Belgrade, the influences don't just come from Istanbul but Vienna, too. Cream slice, krempita, is a perennial favourite, as is Sachertorte. Gesten pure, a chestnut purée which appears as gestenyepüré in every Budapest confectioner's, is another hangover from the Habsburg days. The house speciality remains the Pelivan kolach, a chocolate cake of vanilla cream, hazelnuts, biscuit and white chocolate.

Some twenty flavours of ice cream generate a brisk take-away trade, but the real atmosphere lies inside and the queues on Saturday and Sunday mornings are testament to Pelivan's enduring popularity o

PM Bröd & Sovel

Växjö, Sweden

⚲ Norrgatan 23, 352 31
Växjö, Sweden
↟ pmrestauranger.se

Everything is either home grown or homemade.

Ask anyone in Växjö to point you to the town's best restaurant and they'll direct you to the Michelin-starred PM & Vänner, situated smack in the middle of town. The long established restaurant branched out a few years ago with a state-of-the-art hotel and a café/bakery right next door. As with the restaurant, Per Bengtsson and his fellow owners strove for perfection, which means that the sourdough bread, cakes, pastries and lunch items are out of this world – but prices don't break the bank. The restaurant's mantra 'forest, meadows and lakes' means a policy of serving local Småland produce, and the same philosophy is applied to the bakery. The baked goods are sensational; just behind the counter, you can see the bakers pulling bread from the ovens. Miniature versions of cinnamon buns, cardamom buns and different types of Danish pastries mean you don't have to plump for just one. Patisserie choices change seasonally, but might include chocolate mousse cake, mont blanc and fancy fruit-and-cream-laden tarts. There's also an assortment of pralines. Sandwich fillings and smörrebröd toppings are taken to another level: everything is either home grown or homemade, including marmalades, spreads, vegetables, cured salmon and charcuterie and, as in the restaurant, the majority of the ingredients are organic. The name of the bakery is charming: *bröd* means bread, but even some Swedes don't know that *sovel* means 'leftovers' in the local dialect ⊙

Poilâne

Paris, France

📍 8 rue du Cherche-Midi,
75006 Paris, France
📍 poilane.com

Its sourdough bread has been
an inspiration for many of today's
most dedicated bakers.

Poilâne is known worldwide for its sourdough bread, which has been an inspiration for many of today's most dedicated bakers. The charming premises in St-Germain-des-Prés seem unassuming for such a famous bakery. Take hold of the lovely door handle – fashioned in the shape of an ear of wheat – and step inside the small shop. On either side and in the window are stacked loaves, bread rolls and viennoiserie. This is a boulangerie – there's no patisserie here. What they do have are punitions (punishments) – tempting little shortbread biscuits that melt in the mouth.

At the back of the bakery there's a till and a small counter; in the basement is the wood-fired oven where the bread is baked. Attentive staff deal equally adeptly with dawdling tourists paying homage and brisk 6th arrondissement ladies who shop here every day. The large loaves – sourdough (pain au levain) and rye (pain de seigle) – can be bought whole, or by the half or quarter, sliced or unsliced. Some are covered in splendid raised decorations. There are smaller loaves of walnut (pain aux noix) and sandwich bread (pain de mie).

Now run by the third generation of the Poilâne family, the company also has outlets in London and Antwerp. Also on the rue du Cherche-Midi is Comptoir Poilâne, their tartine café, which serves the bread with a variety of toppings. Of course, Poilâne is now an international brand, with loaves baked elsewhere and sold through supermarkets. Though if you can, it's still worth a visit to the place where it all began ₒ

Pollen Bakery

Manchester, England

Unit 2B, Cotton Field Wharf, 8 New Union Street, Manchester M4 6FQ, England

pollenbakery.com

Viennoiserie includes melt-in-the-mouth croissants (made over four days), along with the likes of cinnamon brioche buns, pain aux raisins and the Saturday speciality, the cruffin.

Having outgrown its bakery-only premises in a railway arch behind Piccadilly station, Pollen migrated to a new space beside the canal in New Islington (part of the Ancoats regeneration area). Customers, many of them young locals, are drawn to the spacious, glass-fronted, concrete-walled bakery/café like bees to a honeypot. Things can get frenetic at weekends, but there's usually space to be found at the long tables to enjoy a short menu of brunch favourites, along with excellent coffee and, of course, brilliant pastries.

Viennoiserie includes melt-in-the-mouth croissants (made over four days), along with the likes of cinnamon brioche buns, pain aux raisins and the Saturday speciality, the cruffin – croissant dough baked in muffin trays and filled with flavoured curd or crème anglaise). Equally delectable is the croissant toast – a croissant sliced then toasted to a crunchy consistency and filled with crème anglaise, fruit, flaked almonds and a dusting of icing sugar. There are cakes too: perhaps an intense salted caramel tart, with a dark biscuitty base and dense, creamy caramel filling, beautifully decorated with chocolate flakes and little pieces of gold leaf; or a crème brûlée tart; or fruit tarts like the one with big, generous chunks of rhubarb on a custard base. Baked cakes such as lemon and poppyseed or raspberry and pistachio also feature.

This is still a business with bread at the core, though; the bakery is at the back, and the loaves turned out by owners Hannah Calvert and Chris Kelly are magnificent. It's all sourdough, made with naturally occurring yeast and using a long fermentation process, with bread taking around twenty-eight hours to produce. Calvert and Kelly favour a darker crust, caused by the sugars in the grain caramelising on the top of the loaf in the heat of the oven – the result is a crust that's more chewy and sweeter than usual. Variations on the standard 28-Hour Sour include 20 per cent rye and all-rye loaves, a five-seed bread and house speciality the Oat Porridge Sour – baked with oat porridge added to the dough for an extra-creamy texture. Every weekend there's something special, too, with seasonal or different ingredients added to the mix.

Note that Pollen is open from Wednesday to Sunday only, and closes at 4pm, by which time it's pretty much guaranteed that all the bread will be gone •

Popty'r Dref

Dolgellau, Wales

📍 Smithfield Street,
Dolgellau LL40 1ET,
Wales
📞 +44 1341 388006

The traditional sweet breads of North Wales take centre stage here.

Dolgellau's reputation as the beating heart of artisanal produce in North Wales took a bit of a knock when the town's beloved 160-year-old bakery Popty'r Dref closed down back in 2011, after 160 years. Fortunately, 'Popty' popped up again a couple of years later: it was so missed that Meinir Jones and her team took it on. They renovated the shop and slowly but surely rebuilt the diverse fan base that's typical of this particular corner of Snowdonia, where tourists, idealistic city escapees and locals often have very different ideas about what constitutes a bakery. Artisanal is great, yes, but all tastes must be catered for when you're a local bakery, so the traditional sweet breads of North Wales take centre stage here. In fact, Jones says, they don't feel a pressure to climb aboard the sourdough wagon – 'there's no call for it'. Instead, they have yeasted multigrain, wholemeal and seeded loaves alongside crusty white bloomers, all baked fresh daily and affordable enough to be indulged in daily.

The Popty thing has always been honeybuns, or more accurately, hynibyns. The original bakery was famous for them, so Jones uses the recipe that came with the shop to make the hynibyn great again. She says that in the days when every street had its own bakery, every bakery had its own take on the hynibyn, made with sweet dough (but no honey), and a comforting accompaniment to a morning coffee. These days people make free with this Welsh delight, adding honey, butter and fruit, but the ones sold here don't contain honey, or all that much sugar. Other traditional Welsh items displayed seductively in the windows include bara brith – the famous fruit and tea bread – along with its heavier, stickier offspring, pudding bara. The well-curranted Welsh cakes are sugary and deliciously short, with that distinctive melt-in-the-mouth quality.

Other, less Welsh, but nevertheless popular confections include cinnamon or raspberry swirls, the chocolate and custard slice and huge, doughy Chelsea buns. The comfortable little café does a brisk trade with its puffy pizza slices and flaky sausage rolls, and is hard to leave on a cold, wet Welsh day ◦

St Ives Bakery

St Ives, England

52 Fore Street, St Ives, Cornwall TR26 1HE, England

stivesbakery.co.uk

Cornish pasty, made with grass-fed beef, local vegetables and a beautiful flaky pasty that falls somewhere delicious between puff and short-crust.

Giant colour-swirled meringues piled in the window signal your arrival at the pint-sized premises of the St Ives Bakery, located just a few paces from the famous bright sands of the harbour beach. Great riches lie within for aficionados of real bread, proper pasties and classic cakes.

The story here is in the detail. Ingredients are carefully sourced (organic Shipton Mill flours, free-range eggs, local raw milk), and no element of the breadmaking is rushed. Each stage of the process is meticulously planned and executed: from beginning to end, St Ives Bakery takes up to thirty-six hours to make a loaf of bread, allowing the bakers to use the lowest possible levels of yeast (as little as 0.06 per cent) and the highest levels of hydration. The bake itself takes place as late as the bakery can possibly manage in order to deliver the bread in its freshest state to the customer. The result of all this is well-out-of-the-ordinary bread possessing both style and substance: moist and springy on the inside, with a very good crust, beautifully scored or seeded.

Aside from the classics such as sourdough, wholemeal, rye and country white, the rosemary-flecked ciabattas and Turkish flatbreads topped with smoky toasted nigella seeds also fly off the shelves. The latter is a salty pleasure that tastes wonderful freshly torn from the bag or spread with a soft goat's cheese.

This is also a fine spot to procure a Cornish pasty, made with grass-fed beef, local vegetables and a beautiful flaky pasty that falls somewhere delicious between puff and short-crust. In summer months there's often a queue snaking out into the road for the likes of the flavour-packed steak and stilton pasty. If pasties aren't your thing, there's a host of sweet offerings: fudge brownies, rock cakes, Bakewell tarts, cookies, bundt cakes and raspberry or chocolate meringues – all baked with the same precision and care as the bread o

St John Bakery

London, England

⦿ 3 Neal's Yard, London WC2H 9DP, England

⤳ stjohnrestaurant.com

This is tradition reimagined into a state of near perfection – not all Eccles cakes are this good, with melt-in-the-mouth pastry and generous, not-too-sweet filling.

Fergus Henderson had a profound and positive effect on London's dining scene when he and Trevor Gulliver opened St John restaurant in 1994, and the St John Bakery has been similarly influential. For years their sourdough loaves and other baked goods were made in one or another of the restaurants, until finally in 2010 a dedicated bakery opened in a railway arch on Druid Street. It supplies the in-house restaurants as well as other shops and cafés, and, as of September 2018, the first standalone St John Bakery shop.

The opening of this small, white unit in Covent Garden makes it much easier for sourdough and doughnut fans to get their fix. The Druid Street premises are open to the public at weekends, but the Neal's Yard outlet is open every day of the week, and it's bang in the centre of town. This is a shop, not a café – there's no room for tables and chairs, just a glass counter filled with loaves and cakes – but there are places to perch in Neal's Yard for customers who can't wait to sample their baked goodies.

As in the restaurants, simplicity and tradition rule the baking – there are no flights of fancy here. Doughnuts come stuffed with the likes of raspberry or blackcurrant jam, with lemon curd, or with vanilla or chocolate custard. Occasionally there's a special – butterscotch, perhaps, or raspberry custard. There are Eccles cakes, individual tarts (custard, Bakewell, lemon curd), cinnamon buns and a small selection of viennoiserie. Before Christmas, there are mince pies. As is the St John way, this is tradition reimagined into a state of near perfection – not all Eccles cakes are this good, with melt-in-the-mouth pastry and generous, not-too-sweet filling. Breads include white and brown sourdough, rye (seeded or plain), raisin loaf, baguette and white tin loaf – the latter ideal for making bacon sandwiches ⦾

© FERGUS HENDERSON

eresa F.R.S For
   Sleepers silk-
cket I can't bear the
 clothes against my
in, likewise if I'm
 feel relaxed and able
 jacket with jeans or
rs and jazzy earrings
eal. (*mytheresa.com*)

k swimsuit is a must,
   for the economical
s among you, wear
 with a pair of high-
and heels.

3 Sunglasses (your choice)
   because they are a must
both for poolside lounging,
and the ideal accompaniment to
a hungover brunch.

4 A night away is a treat. so
   I like to wear my 'best' pjs.
Olivia von Halle is my go to.
(*oliviavonhalle.com*)

5 My gym kit, because in my
   mind's eye, me on a mini-
break is the best version
of myself. I, of course, never use it.
Laura Weir is editor of ES Magazine

BAR · DINING ROOM · WINE S

26 ST. JOHN STR
LONDON

Santo Forno

Florence, Italy

⚲ Via di Santa Monaca 3r,
50124 Florence, Italy
⚓ ilsantobevitore.com

The atmosphere in the vaulted space with its vintage furnishings, unplastered walls and old marble-topped serving counter is still very much intact.

There has been a panificio on the corner of Via dei Serragli and Via Sant'Agostino in the Santo Spirito neighbourhood of Florence's Oltrarno for well over a century. Unlike many bakeries in the city centre, this one had its oven on the premises, so on Sundays, the neighbourhood's oven-less mammas would bring great trays of lasagna and dishes of arrosto (roast meats) to be cooked, then devoured by the family at home.

For forty-odd years, the panificio was owned by Angelo, a Sicilian *fornaio* (baker) who made excellent carciofini ('artichokes' – small, spiky bread rolls) and traditional, salt-free pane Toscano. But in 2014, he sold the business to the dynamic trio behind the hugely popular restaurant Santo Bevitore just around the corner. Marco, Martina and Stefano wanted to offer more than just the traditional breads and cakes found in most Florentine bakeries, so while in the early days Angelo continued to make his tried-and-tested pane Toscano, new, young bakers and pastry chefs were taken on and the choice suddenly became much more interesting.

Wisely, the new owners chose not to over-modernise. The atmosphere in the vaulted space with its vintage furnishings, unplastered walls and old marble-topped serving counter is still very much intact, and mellow background sounds give the place a laid-back vibe. The idea was to introduce a continually evolving roster of baked goods, both sweet and savoury, to keep customers interested: besides the ever-present pane Toscano, pane integrale (wholemeal), crusty sourdough loaves and French-style baguettes, you will find goodies such as rye loaves flavoured with cumin seed, hamburger buns with sesame seeds, walnut and multigrain breads, schiacciata (focaccia), bagels and grissini. The lunch menu (to eat in or take away) includes brilliant seasonally changing quiches encased in flaky, buttery pastry (unusual in Italy), sourdough pizza (classic margherita or the like of potato, grilled aubergine, mozzarella, rocket and confit tomatoes), croque monsieur, seasonal soups and salads. Cakes and pastries are irresistible too – expect frangipane tarts with apricots or pears, 'proper' brownies and cheesecake, carrot cake and banana bread, lemon drizzle and poppy seed cake, lemon chiffon cake with coconut, ricotta tarts and traditional madeleines. All this, and you can still buy Angelo's carciofini ●

Söderberg

Edinburgh, Scotland

27 Simpson Loan,
Edinburgh EH3 9GG,
Scotland
soderberg.uk

Modish Swedish bakery Söderberg has a number of shops and cafés in Edinburgh, but the two within a stone's throw of each other in the upmarket Quartermile district are made for sunny days. Locals flock to the outdoor tables, just off the wide, grassy parkland of the Meadows, to watch a bustling parade of students, cyclists and buskers while sipping a Johan & Nyström latte and savouring one of a range of kardemummabulle (cardamom buns). The delicious, sweet-yet-spicy knotted pastry falls away in satisfying strips and chunks and is perfect for nibbling; Söderberg's varieties come dusted with sugar, stuffed with forest berries or plain. Try the little coconut-encrusted chokladbollar or a slice of moist, chocolatey kladdkaka (mud cake). There are seasonal treats too – rabbit-shaped gingerbread biscuits for Easter, holiday-themed princess cakes in bright coloured marzipan and semla Lenten buns.

Sweden's robust and traditional rye bread (made here with Shipton Mill flour) is the base for a selection of open sandwiches piled high with fillings – the crayfish and boiled egg option is a worthy opponent to the equally tempting smoked salmon and horseradish, both classic tastes of Stockholm. An alternative is the light focaccia with mushrooms and summer vegetables – a satisfyingly chewy snack. A selection of homemade soups and wood-fired sourdough pizzas are also available.

If great food and a perfect people watching position at Simpson Loan aren't enough, wander over to the Pavilion Café branch on Sundays for their late afternoon jazz sessions

Söderberg & Sara

Ystad, Sweden

⚲ 1 Österportstorg, Ystad
271 41, Sweden
⚲ soderbergsara.se

The focus is firmly on Scandinavian breads and grains, such as kavring, a sweet dark rye bread.

The little town of Ystad in Skåne, is best known for an inhabitant who has never lived there: Kurt Wallander, the fictional detective and protagonist of Henning Mankell's murder mystery novels. Ystad is one of the most southerly points in Sweden, and the town faces south across the Baltic towards Denmark and Poland. The real Ystad has a weekend bric-a-brac market, shops selling country wear, and one of Sweden's most renowned coffee roasters and bakeries, Söderberg & Sara.

The bakery is a destination as an eat-in café, for baked goods to take away, and for its excellent coffee roasts. Sourdough baked in a huge stone oven is one of the specialities, made from organic grains milled next door. The focus is firmly on Scandinavian breads and grains, such as kavring, a sweet dark rye bread that is made in the summer and traditionally eaten topped with sill (herring), smoked salmon, pickles or cheese. This kavring rye sourdough is baked in the traditional way inside long hinged tins, and is flavoured with cumin and molasses to give greater depth of flavour. Knotted cardamom or cinnamon buns are also typically Swedish, and are much loved in a country whose main leisure pastime is *fika* – the coffee break. There are also many delectable non-Swedish baked goods, enthusiastically adopted and perfected, such as pasteis de nata, croissants and all manner of carrot and chocolate cakes.

This café is an excellent place for lunch too, as the salads and soups are exemplary; it's a welcome pit stop en route to the sandy beaches of the coast. There is also a branch of Söderberg & Sara in Skåne's main city, Malmö, a 56km drive away. It stocks some of the same baked goods and is also popular, but lacks the remarkable buzz and energy of the Ystad original ◦

Sylvain Depuichaffray

Marseille, France

66 rue Grignan,
13001 Marseille,
France
sylvaindepuichaff
ray.fr

A distinctive style made up of equal parts classicism and informal Aussie-style éclat.

Depuichaffray is regarded by many as the best patissier in Marseille. A former pupil of Pierre Hermé who has worked intensively in Sydney (as well as France, *bien sûr*), he has a distinctive style made up of equal parts classicism and informal Aussie-style éclat. His range of twenty or so patisseries cleaves closely to the standard repertoire – rum baba, Saint Honoré, macaron, chocolate tart – but their realisation, while disciplined, amps up the artistry and provides an all-round sensory appeal. Depuichaffray's signature pastry, a mille feuille in classic and fruity versions, is a good example. From peeling away the confectioner's paper and observing the ooze of vanilla cream and crack of pastry as you apply your fork, to savouring the edge-of-bitter caramel flavour then dusting icing sugar off your lips, it is an experience so sensual that it's hard to believe it's allowed in public.

However, it's not only permitted, it's encouraged. Depuichaffray is as much eaterie as shop, and elevated though its produce might be, the salon de thé is bright and bustling, and welcoming to all-comers. The shopfront divides lengthways into two rooms: one houses the pastry counter, display cases and fridges, where you choose your goodies, and one is the pretty salon with patio-style seating, where you can, if you wish, be served them.

For café lunches and snacks, there's a particularly lovely range of savouries, always including a hot dish, changing specials to reflect the season (for example, salmon and dill on a summer's day), interesting salads and a good range of quiches and savoury tarts.

In the hot Provençal summer, it's almost impossible to resist the house-made ice lollies ('eskimos'), which resemble hand-dipped Magnums and taste amazing. Yet more sweet treats are available around the corner at the new Sylvain Depuichaffray chocolaterie •

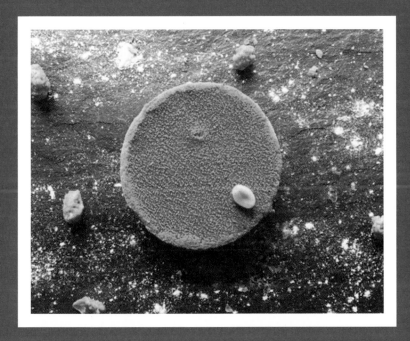

Ten Belles Bread

Paris, France

📍 17-19 rue Bréguet, 75011 Paris, France

📞 +33 1 42 40 90 78

Cakes are a happy cross-Channel exchange.

Ten Belles Bread is a bakery-café, sprung from popular 10th arrondissement café Ten Belles, and sporting a distinctly Anglo-French vibe. Housed on the ground floor of a modern office block, it has an industrial look and a sense of space that's rare in Parisian bakeries. It also has a touch of the London hipster hangout – there are potted plants, a fridgeful of Luscombe fruit juices, good filter coffee in solid mugs, a groovy soundtrack and a pile of English-language cookery books to browse. At the helm are Alice Quillet and Anna Trattles, and their mellow multilingual staff are a friendly bunch.

Bread is baked on site – peek in through the window to see the team at work – and is seriously good, from sourdough through pain de seigle (rye) and pain complet (wholemeal) to focaccia, and there's always a bread of the day (sesame on a recent visit). A favourite

for lunch is one of the heavenly brioche buns; fillings change, but ham, salad and pickles is a typical combo – simple but effective. Every day there's a salad, a toastie, a soup and a few sandwiches on different breads; brunch is served at the weekends. The croque monsieur on sourdough is glorious, and easily enough for two.

Cakes are a happy cross-Channel exchange, and the choice runs from sponges, scones and banana bread to financiers and fancy individual chocolate tarts. Cut through the richness of the latter with an espresso from the gleaming Marzocco machine, with coffee from Belleville Brûlerie (which Anselme Blayney, the third partner in Ten Belles Bread, helped set up). If it's warm enough, enjoy it on the decked area at the back, which overlooks a big modern courtyard ⊚

Tollkötter

Münster, Germany

📍 Prinzipalmarkt 42, 48143
Münster, Germany

🏠 tollkoetter.de

The motto here is 'Tollkötter bakes
something special', and truly, it does.

The first of Theodor
Tollkötter's Münster
bakeries opened its doors
in 1905, and since then,
the family business has
evolved into a much-loved
chain of six outlets around
the city, plus stands at the
weekly markets in Münster
and its Hiltrup suburb. The
motto here is 'Tollkötter
bakes something special',
and truly, it does. Theodor
had a passion for baking,
and his creativity, matched
with his respect for local
baking traditions, were
the foundations for a long-
lived business.

Today, Tollkötter is
run just as enthusiastically
by Konstanze Hanke,
who inherited the business
from her parents. Her
father, Johannes Bundgardt,
developed Tollkötter's
signature loaf, the Tollkötter
Hausbrot, a 7lb rye-mix
sourdough with a crunchy,
inch-thick crust that can
be bought by the loaf or
in single portions. The
Hausbrot has been awarded
a German Agricultural

Society award every year
since it was created in
1976. It is so popular – and
as with many of the other
Tollkötter products, has
such a naturally long shelf
life – that a hundred of
them were once shipped
to Hong Kong. All the baked
goods are of exceptional
quality; the grains –
including old grains such
as emmer, the preservation
of which Bundgardt keenly
supports – come from the
region and are freshly
ground in their own mill.

Fifty different sorts
of bread are baked fresh
each day and sold in the
tiny, friendly bakeries
around Münster's cobbled
central streets. At the shop
on Prinzipalmarkt, the
city's historic marketplace
beautifully reconstructed
after World War II, the
window displays, shelves
and glass counters house
a treasure trove of baked
goods. There are wholegrain
breads, ranging from
Aufreißer®, a crusty rye
baguette, to Fruchtprotz,

a rye and wheat bread
stuffed with apricots, plums
and hazelnuts. The spelt and
wheat bread (Maggiabrot)
has a loose crumb and is
made to an original Italian
recipe; the sweet butter
dough Stuten is filled with
raisins, hazelnuts and
fruits, and decorated with
sugar frosting and hazelnut
leaves. A large number
of the loaves are vegan,
and Tollkötter even has a
separate production site
dedicated to making gluten-
free pastries and buckwheat
and amaranth breads.

In addition to loaves,
there are thirty different
kinds of bread rolls on offer,
including a popular rye
mix sourdough, Knüfchen,
plus a host of cakes and
pastries. Choose from
traditional seasonal German
fruit tray bakes, marble
or eggnog cake, or in the
run-up to Christmas all
manner of Advent cookies,
including Spritzgebäck –
crisp, dry buttery biscuits
– and Tollkötter's famous
gingerbread Printen ⊙

Tössebageriet

Stockholm, Sweden

⚲ Karlavägen 77,
114 49 Stockholm,
Sweden

⚑ tosse.se

For a full-on cream, mousse and custard experience, try the Napoleon.

Tössebageriet, run by Culinary Olympics gold medallist and pastry chef extraordinaire Mattias Ljungberg, is a Stockholm institution, going strong since 1920 and still a trendsetter. Any desire for fine pastries and fancy cakes can be satisfied here. The counter is brimming with all kinds of sweet temptations, from Swedish classics such as princess cake (whipped cream, vanilla custard, raspberry jam and green marzipan) to French-inspired treats like eclairs and tartelettes with seasonal fruits and berries. For a full-on cream, mousse and custard experience, try the Napoleon: a rectangular mille feuille pastry filled with whipped cream, vanilla custard and jam, topped with a sugar glaze flavoured with blackcurrants. The Swedish royal family are fans of Tössebageriet; both the crown princess Victoria and her younger brother Carl Philip ordered their wedding cakes from 'Tösse'.

The shop is located in Östermalm, Stockholm's most affluent neighbourhood, but the ambiance is anything but snobbish, and the service is always warm and smiling – even when the queue to get one of the legendary semlor (cardamom buns with cream and almond paste filling) is trailing around the block. Despite its old school charm, Tössebageriet was at the

centre of cake controversy a few years ago, when Ljungberg made a modern twist on the traditional semlor. All he did was fashion them in the form of a more easily eaten wrap, but seldom has the semlor season (January–March) seen such heated discussion. To the traditionalists dismay, the 'semmelwrap' has prevailed and is much copied, but this is its place of origin ⊙

Tout Autour du Pain

Paris, France

⌖ 59 rue de Saintonge, Paris 75003, France
☏ no phone

The schwartzbrot is a joyous find for anyone who likes a dense bread with plenty of taste.

A showcase for the talents of Benjamin Turquier, Tout Autour du Pain is a bakery with two outlets, just a street apart. This one, on the rue de Saintonge, isn't huge, but it has room for a few seats where you can perch with a croissant and a coffee, and there's a bakery at the back; the other outlet on the rue de Turenne is tiny, and any queue quickly snakes out of the door. The two branches close on different days, so one or the other is always open.

People come here for the bread – the choice is more varied than in most French bakeries, even in Paris. The schwartzbrot is a joyous find for anyone who likes a dense bread with plenty of taste; it's equally good on its own with butter, or toasted. It's sold here in various sizes, but buy more than you think you need as it lasts for ages. There are many other loaves, running in style from the deservedly award-winning baguette to a pain baltik.

Viennoiserie come in regular and mini versions. The pain aux raisins is beautifully moist, while the chocolate chip brioche and the bite-size chouquettes are equally irresistible. There are madeleines, eclairs, pretty fruit tarts (raspberry, strawberry), individual lemon and chocolate tarts, and cheesecake, too. Savouries include a range of small quiches, plus sandwiches, filled baguettes and a cheesy bread roll. Also crammed in are a few store cupboard items such as coffee and honey. Try to scope out what you want to order before you get to the head of the queue – service can be a little brusque ●

Trove

Manchester, England

9 1032 Stockport Road,
Manchester M19 3WX,
England
⚑ trovefoods.co.uk

Sourdoughs, white and
wholemeal, have big
flavours with sweet, tangy
crusts and moist insides.

Trove is big draw on out-of-the-way Levenshulme's main drag. It's full all day at weekends, with customers travelling miles to reach the place and then willing to wait for a table for brunch or lunch. But it's the brilliant bread – famous locally and sold at various locations around Manchester as well as at the café – that's the foundation of their success. It's unsullied by artificial ingredients: sourdough loaves rise by means of natural yeast alone and use of other yeast is kept to a minimum in all products; flour is organic and stone-ground; flour improvers and the like are out. Time is invested in the loaves, with each taking a minimum of sixteen hours from mixing the pre-ferments, which are left for twelve hours, to loaves finally emerging from the oven. Resulting sourdoughs, white and wholemeal, have big flavours with sweet, tangy crusts and moist insides. Other loaves are equally splendid, and there's a great range: white bloomer, wholemeal molasses and sunflower seed, rye and fennel, plus baguettes and ciabattas.

Cakes – served in very generous portions in the café – include creative bakes, such as Persian cake (a soft, yellow sponge made moist by rosewater and topped with pistachio), plus twists on more traditional cakes, like the ginger Bakewell tarts. They sit on a counter in the front of the low key but welcoming Scandi-look premises, all white walls and blonde-wood furnishings. There's more seating at the back, along with an open kitchen.

Baked goods aside, the café majors on brunch, with winning global combos such as spicy merguez sausages offset by smooth, silky labneh, plus fried egg, carrot and kohrabi; or a tofu, kimchi, kale, chilli and sesame rice bowl. There are classics too, like eggs benedict, and a vegan breakfast (here a kind of posh full English, with mushrooms, polenta, greens, cannellini beans, chutney and toast). Coffee is from Allpress. Trove has expanded into limited evening openings, featuring small plates, cocktails, organic wines and craft beers, and – of course – cakes from the counter ⊙

Ugga

Amsterdam, Netherlands

📍 Gerard Doustraat 103 A, 1073 VS Amsterdam, Netherlands

↳ ugga.nl

The babkas are great favourites: these cake-breads come in many guises, such as chocolate, lemon, ricotta and raisin, or savoury ones such as sun-dried tomato, spinach and goats cheese.

These cosy premises in the lively De Pijp district are home to Ugga, a self-styled 'urban bakery' owned by Adva Rachamim. Originally from Israel, Adva trained at the French Pastry School in Chicago, and then worked as a pastry chef at several restaurants in Amsterdam before taking the leap to open her own business in 2017. She makes all the goodies in the shop herself, and pays great attention to presentation, too – the counter display looks a treat. The interior is small, but bright and full of light, and there are a few seats for eating in.

Ugga is Hebrew for cake; the tempting selection of regular bakes is supplemented by enough specials to keep things interesting: variations on sufganiyot (jam-filled doughnuts for Hanukkah) or hamantaschen (triangular pastries filled with fruit preserve for Purim); or a succession of croffins. The babkas are great favourites: these cake-breads come in many guises, such as chocolate, lemon, ricotta and raisin, or savoury ones such as sun-dried tomato, spinach and goats cheese. Croissants come plain or filled, and there's an ever-changing choice of topped focaccia. There's challah (egg-enriched dough, in plain, spelt, poppyseed and sesame seed varieties) every Friday; there might be pita za'atar (made with fresh za'atar – similar to oregano) and ungainly looking bagels. Cakes can also be made to order for special occasions.

Other must-tries are the rugalach (like a croissant but softer) and the burekas (thin flaky pastry, here open or rolled), with different fillings, such as tomato, basil and mozzarella. Get there early in the morning to sample them straight out of the oven ⊚

Violet

London, England

📍 47 Wilton Way, London
E8 3ED, England
🔗 violetcakes.com

What keeps devotees loyal is the inventiveness and the seasonality.

Although well known to east Londoners and *Guardian* readers (American owner Claire Ptak had a column in the paper), Violet reached another level of fame when it was announced that the bakery would be providing Prince Harry and Meghan Markle's non-traditional wedding cake (lemon and elderflower). But anyone expecting grand premises will be disappointed: the two-storey, white-painted building is small and unassuming. The ground floor has a tiny kitchen/bakery, a till point, a coffee machine and a cabinet of baked goodies. Your eye is instantly drawn to the tidy rows of immaculate cupcakes, topped with buttercream in an ever-changing set of flavours. The namesake violet flavour is a delicate must-try, though the lemon is pretty special too; it's hard to choose, but they come in bite-sized sizes, so you can easily sample more than one. Order at the counter

and make your way to seats upstairs or outside.

What keeps devotees loyal is the inventiveness and the seasonality: upside-down almond polenta American muffins with blood orange and clotted cream, blondies, halva brownies, vanilla custard rhubarb tarts. The style is closer to domestic baking than the glazed perfection of the professional patisserie, but the cakes taste so much better than most people can achieve at home. The special occasion cakes are indeed fit for a princess: made to order, the tiered sponge cakes are covered in buttercream and decorated with flowers, and come in flavours such as coconut or chocolate violet cream (there are also vegan and gluten-free options).

Like the sweet stuff, the baked savouries are made with quality ingredients, organic where possible. There are deep-filled quiches (Serrano ham with comté cheese, or

potato, caramelised onion and cheddar), and American biscuits (more like a savoury scone) with bacon and egg. There are always fresh ideas on the café menu too: a list of gooey toasties made with bread from nearby e5 Bakehouse includes one with cheddar, blue cheese and kimchi, served with sweet jelly and pickles. A good range of drinks includes JARR kombucha, own-made lemonade, coffee roasted by Allpress and loose-leaf teas from Postcard Teas ●

The Wee Boulangerie

Edinburgh, Scotland

⚐ 67 Clerk Street,
Edinburgh EH8 9JG,
Scotland

⚑ theweeboulangerie.co.uk

Leave room for at least one of the beautifully buttery croissants.

The owners of this French bakery and patisserie – nestled cheek by jowl among the independent shops and cafés of Clerk Street – weren't just being cute when they chose the name. The premises can only accommodate a maximum of six customers around a handful of scrubbed wooden tables. For everyone else, including a steady stream of loyal locals who have been won over by the delicious breads and snacks, a quick take-away must suffice.

If you miss the early lunchtime rush for the soup of the day (accompanied, of course, by a hunk of the Boulangerie's own crusty loaf), you're best choosing between a summery pizzetta – a mini-pizza topped with an ever-changing menu of toppings – or a fougasse, a soft, olive oil bread, here stuffed with different fillings (halloumi with artichoke is a treat). Focaccia bites and a variety of quiches are also available.

The sweet stuff is just as delectable – the chocolate bun is a pain au lait laced with a rich seam of dark chocolate (à la pain au chocolat) and topped with a decorative row of Mohican-like spikes that pop satisfyingly between your teeth. Somewhat less sugary – but just as tasty – are the fruit tartlets. Their moist, sticky fillings are surrounded by soft and not-too-crumbly pastry case. If you're feeling particularly French, you can also purchase a small box of colourful macarons.

The breads on offer start at the lighter end of the scale – baguettes, French whites – and extend to dense loaves of rye bread and sourdough (scheduled bake times are published on social media so you can arrive to collect them fresh from the oven). And – since no French bakery would be complete without them – make sure you leave room for at least one of the beautifully buttery croissants ⊙

Rye Bre

Weichardt

Berlin, Germany

⚲ Mehlitzstraße 7, 10715 Berlin, Germany
⚲ weichardt.de

It's a wonderfully traditional, cosy shop, all wooden shelves and brown floor tiles.

You'll find plenty of hip, modern bakeries all over Berlin, but for high quality bread, and a commitment to craftsmanship and tradition, it's unlikely you'll find a better one than Weichardt. Berlin's first wholemeal bakery was founded in 1977 by pastry and dessert chef Heinz Weichardt, who had been repeatedly approached by friends and acquaintances who complained about the lack of wholegrain bread in Berlin. He began by baking at a friend's cake shop after work, selling the loaves on the street outside local kindergartens with his wife Mucke; the successful family business is now run by their daughter, Yvonne, who oversees their three bakeries and a café.

Weichardt's main location in Berlin's south-western borough of Wilmersdorf opened in 1981, following extensive soundproofing of the site to prevent their three stone mills from disturbing the building's other tenants. It's a wonderfully traditional, cosy shop, all wooden shelves and brown floor tiles, with seating both inside and out, and it's much loved for its lively atmosphere. From the shop floor you can see directly into the production area, where all the Weichardt breads, cakes and pastries continue to be made each day: regular customers stop in for breakfast just so they can feel like part of the action.

Weichardt has been using the same organic ingredients, methods and traditional recipes since the beginning. Their 100 per cent wholegrain flour, butter and honey come from Demeter-approved farms (Demeter, the world's largest certification organisation for biodynamic agriculture, was founded in Berlin in 1928), and they work with their own natural sourdough starter. 'Things that should be good, really need time,'

says Heinz, and he means it: each loaf of bread takes a full twenty-four hours to make. Try the Leinsamen-Weizenschrotbrot (flaxseed shredded wheat bread), the first wholegrain bread Heinz ever baked, or choose one of the other classic German loaves from Weichardt's small selection – they're focused on quality, not quantity here.

Weichardt also offers a good range of traditional German cakes and pastries, from Käsekuchen (cheesecake) and Mohnkuchen (poppyseed cake), to Streusel (crumble cake) and Bienenstich (bee sting cake), plus some of Heinz's own favourites, Schokosahnetorte (chocolate torte) and Schweineohren (palmiers). At Eastertime, chocolate rabbits are made by hand and beautifully wrapped in cellophane and ribbons; come summer, you'll find strawberry and plum cakes aplenty. In the run up to Christmas, the shelves are weighed down with all the Weichardt Christmas favourites, including Stollen, Baumkuchen (German 'spit' cake) and Honigkuchen (honey cake, the base dough for which is begun in April), not to mention chocolate Father Christmases, marzipan and a choice selection of nut pralines. The chocolate-covered honey cake hearts dotted with almonds make a lovely traditional Christmas gift ∘

Yann Couvreur

Paris, France

9 23 bis rue des Rosiers,
75004 Paris, France

↟ yanncouvreur.com

The cakes look like glistening
jewels and the flavours change
with the seasons.

Yann Couvreur is a young, modish pastry chef, producing striking and precise creations in three central sites: this one, close to the falafel shops of the Marais, opened in 2017; the first, in the 10th arrondissement, opened in 2016; and a third, the YC Café at Galeries Lafayette Gourmet on boulevard Haussmann, in 2018. In this small space in the Marais, there are a few stools at a long counter, opposite an equally long glass case containing the patisserie, pastries and chocolates. A coffee machine is squeezed into one corner, and there are juices and a few lunch items too. It's impossible not to focus on the patisserie though: the cakes look like glistening jewels and the flavours change with the seasons; eclair caraïbe is a neat, glistening rectangle of loveliness, covered in milk chocolate and coconut flecks. A vanilla fraisier (sponge cake) comes covered with discs of sliced strawberry, while the baba is topped by whipped cream dotted with raspberries and fresh mint. The flavours aren't necessarily traditional, but they're always well-conceived and worth trying.

The viennoiserie is no afterthought – the kouglof, dotted with flaked almonds and candied fruit, are divine, a bun you could happily eat every day. As well as croissants and pains au chocolat, there are a selection of roulé (rolled pastries in different flavours), chouquettes flavoured with orange blossom, and kouign amann made with buckwheat. A small range of chocolates includes some covetable examples in the shape of sleeping foxes – the fox being the motif of the shop.

Aside from the talent and the artistry, what's so refreshing about this patisserie is that it's a relaxing, friendly place to be – it's not pretentious or intimidating, and you really can perch at the wooden counter and just have a coffee and a croissant. Maybe one day all Parisian patisseries will be this welcoming ◦

CRE

DITS

Credits

Review contributors

Ashleigh Arnott, Ismay Atkins, Timothy Bird, Caroline Bishop, Niki Boyle, Marti Buckley, Kate Carlisle, Peterjon Cresswell, Christi Dietz, Guy Dimond, Claire Doble, Anne Faber, Sarah Guy, Ronnie Haydon, Andrew Humphreys, Lena Ilkjær, Ruth Jarvis, Kathryn Kelly, Robert Martin, Anna Norman, Ros Sales, Mathias Steinbru, Nicky Swallow, Valerie Waterhouse.

Photo credits

We'd like to thank all the bakeries, the review contributors above and an international legion of Instagrammers who provided the photographs for this book.

Every effort has been made to find the correct copyright holder. Please contact us so we can rectify any issues on info@septemberpublishing.org.

pp. 2–3 Leve: Apelöga; p. 7 Pastas Beatriz: Raquel Idoate, @raqueliodoate; p. 7 Pastéis de Belém: Antiga Confeitaria de Belém, Lda; p. 7 Meyers: Stine Christiansen; p. 7 Gragger: Daniela Wiebogen; p. 7 Maison Dandoy: Maison Dandoy; p. 7 Patisserie Sainte Anne: Chiho Cookson, @gipcy_art_chee; p. 7 Gerbeaud: Gerbeaud Gasztronomia Ltd; p. 7 Åpent Bakeri: Ösp Egilsdóttir; p. 7 Black Isle Bakery: Robert Rieger; p. 7 Bageriet: Nick Selby; p. 7 Meyers: Stine Christiansen; p. 7 Violet: Claire Ptak; p. 8 Meyers: Anders Schønnemann; p. 12 Åpent Bakeri: Åpent Bakeri, p. 13, top Åpent Bakeri: Maike Hertel Ergo, bottom Åpent Bakeri: Ösp Egilsdóttir; p. 14 Aran: Roddy Hand 2018; p. 15 Aran: Roddy Hand 2018; p. 16 Aromat: Maciej Stanik for Melting Pot Sp. Z O.O.; p. 17 Aromat: Maciej Stanik for Melting Pot Sp. Z O.O.; p. 18 Auguszt: Flora Auguszt; p. 19 Bäckerei Balkhausen: Brigitte Girmann, @briduettchen; p. 20 Bäckerei Hinkel: Michael Lübke for Bäckerei Hinkel; p. 21 Bäckerei Hinkel: Michael Lübke for Bäckerei Hinkel; p. 22 Bäckerei Pfeifle: Michael Schulze, @brotbruder_fr; p. 23 Bageri Petrus: Megan Quick, @mquickness; p. 24 Bageriet: Nick Selby; p. 25 Bageriet: Nick Selby; p. 26 Baker Tom: Adam Sargent; p. 27 Baker Tom: Adam Sargent; p. 28 Baker's Table at Talgarth Mill: Talgarth Mill; p. 29 Bakeshop: Bakeshop; p. 30

Baltic Bakehouse: Shannon McConkey, @instashan92; p. 31 Barbakan: Aimee Peace; p. 32 Beigel Bake: Daisy Malivoire, @daisymalivoirephoto; p. 33 Bertinet Bakery Café: Bertinet Bakery Café; p. 34 Bettys: Bettys; p. 35 Bettys: Bettys; p. 36 Bewley's: Barry Mccall; p. 37 Bewley's: Holly Montell; p. 39 Biscottificio Antonio Mattei: Laura Meffe; p. 40 Black Isle Bakery: Robert Rieger; p. 41 Black Isle Bakery: Robert Rieger; p. 42 Blé: Elizabet Yordanova, @elizabethyordanova; p. 43 A Blikle: A Blikle; p. 44 Bougatsa Giannis: Guy Dimond; p. 45 Bread Ahead: Frida Thelin; p. 46 Bread Source: Luke W. Bryant; p. 47 Bread Station: @jennifermoseleychef; p. 48 Brotgarten: Milena Zwerenz, @milenazwerenz; p. 51 Caffè Sicilia: Francesco Di Martino; p. 52 Café Succès: Anders Backman; p. 53 Café Succès: Anders Backman; p. 55 La Campana: Cristina Ponay, @kitina; p. 57 Casa Aranda: Gosia Baziak, @misbadu_official; p. 58 Chambelland: Mick Jayet and Maud Bernos; p. 59 Chambelland: Mick Jayet and Maud Bernos; p. 60 Chatzis: Guy Dimond; p. 61 Companio Bakery: Clare Fogden, @scuttlerclare; p. 63 Comptoir Gourmand: @koshhussain; p. 64 ConditCouture: Jens Iwan Schoenfelder; p. 65 ConditCouture: Jens Iwan Schoenfelder; p. 66 Conditorei Péclard im Schober: Raphael Otto; p. 67 Conditorei Péclard im Schober: Jason Lioh, @jasonlioh; p. 68 Conditori La Glace: Tea Tougaard, @teatougaard.dk; p. 69 Conditori Nordpolen: Håkan Göthberg, @hakangothberg; p. 70 Confiserie Graff: @vineatscake; p. 71 Cookie Jar: Kathryn Kelly; p. 72 Cottonrake Bakery: Daniel Dewolfe; p. 73 Cottonrake Bakery: Daniel Dewolfe; p. 74 Cukrárna Myšák: Filip Šlapal; p. 75 Cukrárna Myšák: Honza Zima; p. 77 Damniczki: Edina Galyas, @edinagalyas; p. 78 Demel: Demel Wien; p. 79 Demel: Demel Wien; p. 80 Det Rene Brød: Susan Champlin, @susanchamplin; p. 81 Dominique Ansel: Scott Grumett; p. 82 Du Pain et des Idées: Benoît Linero; p. 83 Du Pain et des Idées: Benoît Linero; p. 84 Dusty Knuckle Bakery: Anton Rodriguez; p. 85 Dusty Knuckle Bakery: Anton Rodriguez; p. 86 e5 Bakehouse: Helen Cathcart; p. 87 e5 Bakehouse: Helen Cathcart; p. 88 Earth's Crust: Kim Ayres; p. 89 Earth's Crust: Kim Ayres; p. 90 left Ekberg: Wendy Erasmus, South Africa, @wendy_erasmus, right Ekberg: Janina Havia, @janinakatriinahavia; p. 91 Fabrica Das Verdadeiras Queijadas Da Sapa:

@maria.abreulobo; **p.** 92 Falko: Falko Bakery; **p.** 93 Falko: Falko Bakery; **p.** 94 Farinoman: Tamsin Davies, @t_davies; **p.** 95 Fazer Café: Arooma Gul, @aroomagul; **p.** 96 Flint Owl Bakery: David Bland; **p.** 97 Flint Owl Bakery: David Bland; **p.** 98 Il Fornaio di Domenica Ordine: Selene Oddenino; **p.** 99 La Fougasse d'Uzès: La Fougasse d'Uzès; **p.** 100 Gerbeaud: Gerbeaud Gasztronomia Ltd; **p.** 101 Gerbeaud: Gerbeaud Gasztronomia Ltd; **p.** 102 *top* Gragger: Daniela Wiebogen, *bottom* Gragger: Saša Asanović; **p.** 103 Güntherska Hovkonditori & Schweizeri: Niklas Lundengård, Destination Uppsala; **p.** 104 Hambleton Bakery: Hambleton Bakery; **p.** 105 Hambleton Bakery: Hambleton Bakery; **p.** 106 Hartog's Volkoren: Fred Tiggelman; **p.** 107 Hartog's Volkoren: Fred Tiggelman; **p.** 108 Haxby Bakehouse: Tony Bartholomew; **p.** 109 Haxby Bakehouse: Tony Bartholomew; **p.** 110 Hobbs House Bakery: Dan Jevons; **p.** 111 Hobbs House Bakery: Dan Jevons; **p.** 112 Hofbäckerei Edegger-Tax: Anna Arkushyna, @mrsannnna; **p.** 113 Hofbäckerei Edegger-Tax: Hofbäckerei Edegger-Tax; **p.** 114 Hofpfisterei: Dobránska Renáta, Stocksy; **p.** 116 Ille Brød: Jon-Are Berg-Jacobsen; **p.** 117 Ille Brød: Jon-Are Berg-Jacobsen; **p.** 118 Isabella Glutenfreie Patisserie: Sabrina Weniger; **p.** 120 Korica: Hoi Polloi D.O.O.; **p.** 121 Kruščić: Peterjon Cresswell; **p.** 122 Lanskroon: Eric Poffers; **p.** 123 Lanskroon: Eric Poffers; **p.** 124 Leakers: Rob@Eatpictures; **p.** 125 Levain: Tuukka Koski; **p.** 126 Leve: Apelöga; **p.** 127 Leve: Måns Jensen; **p.** 128 The Loaf: Marta Etxebarria Photography, @martaetxebarria; **p.** 129 The Loaf: Marta Etxebarria Photography, @martaetxebarria; **p.** 130 Lukullus: Jacek Malarski; **p.** 131 Lukullus: Jacek Malarski; **p.** 132 Maison Adam: David-Duchon-Doris; **p.** 133 Maison Adam: David-Duchon-Doris; **p.** 134 Maison Aleph: Caspar Miskin; **p.** 135 Maison Aleph: Caspar Miskin; **p.** 136 *top* Maison Dandoy: Lydie Nesvadba, *bottom* Maison Dandoy: Maison Dandoy; **p.** 137 Maison Dandoy: Maison Dandoy; **p.** 139 Maison Villaret: Ruth Jarvis, @ruth_jarvis; **p.** 141 Maison Violette: Ruth Jarvis, @ruth_jarvis; **p.** 143 Maison Weibel: Studio Aq; **p.** 144 Mali Princ: Petra Berende; **p.** 145 Manteigaria: Guy Dimond; **p.** 147 Marchesi 1824: Maria Lucia Vestrucci, @cupmallows; **p.** 148 La Marquise: La Marquise; **p.** 149 McKee's Country Store: Kathryn Kelly; **p.** 150 Meyers Bakery: Stine Christiansen; **p.** 151 Meyers Bakery: Stine Christiansen; **p.** 152 *top* Moser's Backparadies: Natalie_Barth/ Shutterstock.com, *bottom* Moser's Backparadies Elena Gargiulo Khelil, @elena_khelil; **p.** 154 Namur: Marianne Nickels & Claudine Bossler; **p.** 155 Oberweis: Studio des Fleurs, Laurent Fau; **p.** 156 Old Post Office Bakery: Maider Jiménez; **p.** 157 Old Post Office Bakery: Maider Jiménez; **p.** 158 Olof Viktors Bageri och Café: Klas

Andersson; **p.** 159 Olof Viktors Bageri och Café: Klas Andersson; **p.** 160 Padaria Ribeiro: Sandra Voigt-Müller, @sandrazuna; **p.** 161 Panella Roma: Juri Pozzi, Stocksy; **p.** 162 Panificio Bonci: Natalie Kennedy, @anamericaninrome; **p.** 163 Panificio Constantini: Stefano Mazzola/Shutterstock.com; **p.** 165 Panificio Davide Longoni: Diletta Sereni for Panificio Davide Longoni; **p.** 166 Panificio Mario: Luca Amodeo, @luca_amodeo1; **p.** 167 Parémi: Sakina Viaphay, @sakinav; **p.** 168 Pariés: Ambre Gaudet, @48hchrono; **p.** 169 Pastas Beatriz: Raquel Idoate, @raqueliodoate; **p.** 171 Pastéis de Belém: Antiga Confeitaria de Belém, Lda; **p.** 172 Pastelería Arrese: Pastelería Arrese; **p.** 173 Pastelería Oiartzun: Gemma Monter, @gemma_says; **p.** 175 Patisserie Holtkamp: Jeroen Vd Spek; **p.** 176 Patisserie Sainte Anne: Chiho Cookson, @gipcy_art_chee; **p.** 177 Patisserie Tarte & Törtchen: Harald Greiner, @haraldgreiner; **p.** 178 Pékműhely: Pékműhely; **p.** 179 Pékműhely: Pékműhely; **p.** 180 Pelivan: Petra Berende; **p.** 181 PM Bröd & Sovel: PM Bröd & Sovel; **p.** 182 Poilâne: Poilâne®; **p.** 183 Poilâne: Poilâne®; **p.** 185 Pollen Bakery: Chris Kelly; **p.** 186 Popty'r Dref: Lowri Haf Cooke, @lowrihafcooke; **p.** 187 St Ives Bakery: Giulia Mule, @mondomulia; **p.** 188 St John Bakery: Gabriella Delgado-Rhodes, @swissmunchkinsdishes; **p.** 189 St John Bakery: Andra Constantinescu, @mintandrosemary; **p.** 191 Santo Forno: Marina Denisova; **p.** 193 Söderberg: Dario Rodrigues; **p.** 194 Söderberg & Sara: Per Söderberg; **p.** 195 Söderberg & Sara: Per Söderberg; **p.** 197 Sylvain Depuichaffray: Leïla Ait-yala, @massifoodies; **p.** 198 Ten Belles: Paperclip Images, Stocksy; **p.** 199 Ten Belles Bread: Miquel Llonch, Stocksy; **p.** 201 Tolkötter: Leila Prousch, @muenstermama; **p.** 202 Tössebageriet: adrenalinerushdiaries/Shutterstock.com; **p.** 203 Tout Autour du Pain: Jérémie Dubois; **p.** 204 Trove: Jordan Davis & Willie Runte; **p.** 205 Trove: Jordan Davis & Willie Runte; **p.** 206 *top* Ugga: Gerrit Basson, *bottom* Ugga: Nima Ghorbani; **p.** 207 Ugga: Gerrit Basson; **p.** 208 Violet: Claire Ptak; **p.** 209 Violet: Kristin Perers; **p.** 210 *top* The Wee Boulangerie: Naomi Smith, *bottom* The Wee Boulangerie: Amandine Butticaz; **p.** 211 The Wee Boulangerie: Amandine Butticaz; **p.** 213 Weichardt: Ina Peters, Stocksy; **p.** 214 Yann Couvreur: Laurent Fau; **p.** 215 Yann Couvreur: Laurent Fau; **p.** 218–19 Aran: Roddy Hand 2018; **p.** 221 Leve: Måns Jensen; **p.** 222 Yann Couvreur: Laurent Fau; **p.** 224 Black Isle Bakery: Robert Rieger.

Additional acknowledgements

Sarah Guy would also like to thank: Petra Berende, Sally Davies, Kei Ishimaru, Max Krauss-Waller, Justin McDonnell, Jenni Muir, Raluca Micu, Yolanda Zappaterra.

From the fields of Mount Eagle search the skies for the Red Kite.